THE FI TRAVELER

How to See More of the World for Less

by

Caroly Jones

FIRST EDITION

Newjoy Press
Ventura, California U.S.A.

THE FRUGAL TRAVELER
How to See More
of the World for Less
by

Caroly Jones

Published by
   Newjoy Press
   Post Office Box 3437
   Ventura, California 93006 U.S.A.
   800-876-1373
   Fax: 805-984-0503
   E-mail: njpublish@aol.com

© 2000 by Caroly Jones
   Printed in the United States of America

Cataloging in Publication Data

Jones, Caroly
   The Frugal Traveler: How to See More of the World for Less
   Includes a bibliography and an index
1.   Travel: Frugal
2.   Economical Travel
3.   Adventure Travel

LCCN: 98-65290

ISBN: 1-879899-16-7   **$15.95**

DEDICATION

For George

*Whose taste for adventure has seasoned
and enriched our life together.*

TABLE OF CONTENTS

DISCLAIMER

This book is designed to provide helpful information about the subject matter covered. It is sold with the understanding that the publisher and author are not engaged in rendering professional travel services by means of this book

Every effort has been made to make this book as complete and accurate as possible. However, there may be mistakes, both typographic and in content. Therefore, this text should be used only as a general guide, and not as the ultimate source of travel information. Furthermore, this book contains information on travel only up to the printing date.

The purpose of this book is to educate and entertain. The author and Newjoy Press shall have neither liability nor responsibility to any person or entity with respect to any loss or damage caused, or alleged to be caused, directly or indirectly, by the information contained in this book.

If you do not wish to be bound by the above, you may return this book to the publisher for a full refund.

ABOUT THE AUTHOR

Caroly Jones and her husband, George, live in the mountains of western New Mexico on their twenty-acre Ranchito Chupaflor. It is named for the hundreds of hummingbirds that visit them each summer.

The author has been a teacher, a public relations director, and a freelance writer. She has published articles about a variety of subjects, many of them related to her own life. She wrote about divorces when she got one, and traveling when she was able to do some.

She wrote this book because she and George learned so much about traveling inexpensively in many parts of the world. She wants to share this knowledge with others interested in venturing forth.

Caroly's next book may be about her current project—building an adobe house from the ground up. She and George are living in an RV while they work on it. They expect to have it completed in 2000.

Caroly and George have traveled during the past three winters, going frugally to Baja California, Hawaii, Australia and Southeast Asia. They also travel in the U.S. Summers find them canoeing down rivers, hiking in the mountains and camping whenever they can.

ACKNOWLEDGMENTS

Thanks in particular to my writers' group, an informal gathering of four women. We met weekly over a period of several years to review each other's work. The final version of this book is a product of the attention given to it by three marvelous women, who are excellent and published writers. Thank you Gloria Mallory, Mary Kirschner, and April Kopp.

My family, too, has been helpful, encouraging and supportive throughout the ten-year process of creating a long and cumbersome first effort, the process of submitting to major presses and universal rejections, refocusing and rewriting, more marketing, more rejections, small press marketing and finally, success. My mother and her friends at La Vida Llena gave me a needed lift. "It will be a best seller," they generously said after reading the final manuscript. "I've got goosebumps," claimed one of our three terrific daughters after hearing the book had been sold.

George gets the biggest thank-you for putting food on the table and money in the bank when the earnings from my freelance writing were in the triple digits.

I may not make a pile of money from this book to compensate me for the effort involved, but the satisfaction from having brought the project to completion and publication is incalculable. Thank you, Joy, for taking a chance on *The Frugal Traveler*.

INTRODUCTION

During the 50s, I grew up in a family that regarded travel as one of the basic food groups. When Daddy had his two weeks off every summer, we hopped in the Ford and left Ohio. We slept in $4-a-night roadside cabins, Mom fried hamburgers in kitchenette skillets on hot plates, and my brother and I fought over the blanket in a saggy double bed. We often got as far as Canada, where we rented rustic cottages on cold, clear lakes. Sometimes there was a rowboat.

These family vacations brought adventure and even magic into our lives. I didn't know it then, but those trips made me assume travel would forever be an important and necessary part of my life. This assumption set me up for problems later when I married a person who preferred doing something else with his vacation besides travel—such as compete in handball tournaments.

And so, after a divorce, I eventually married someone who shared my passion for travel. I decided he was the man for me on our first date, when he told me that when he was 19, he and

1

a friend got into a 1960 Ford Falcon and drove from Florida to Alaska. Then they drove to Costa Rica—then Nova Scotia. The car was completely used up, he said. I was completely smitten.

We have been frugal travelers together ever since—exploring the world, developing our skills, and visiting countries on five continents in the process.

Why frugal travel as opposed to normal, everyday travel? For one simple reason—the less we spend, the more often we can afford to go. Travel is at the top of our list of what we want to do with discretionary income. We would no more squander two or three years worth of travel money on one lavish two-week trip than we would allow ourselves to pay interest on the MasterCard account. (Frugal here, frugal there.) For us, there's much more world to see than there is time. We want to get in as much as we can.

Not everyone shares this attitude. A majority of Americans prefer to vacation rather than travel. They want their time away from home to be more comfortable than challenging. A trip, they reason, should be carefree and relaxing. This is why, if they venture abroad at all, most Americans go on tours. It's easier. Independent travel is *not* easy. In fact, it requires a fair amount of effort. Frugal independent travel is even tougher.

Many Americans say if they had more time and/or money they would like to travel, but few act on these desires. The American attitude toward foreign travel reminds me of what writing teachers observe about their students. Most of them want to be published more than they want to write. Similarly, many people would love to have gone to a variety of exotic destinations, but they don't actually want to undertake the trip.

This choice is understandable. Travel of any sort is disruptive, exhausting and disorienting. Yet those who love to travel have learned that, like writing, the act itself provides its own rewards. It is not important, finally, to have been to Katmandu, Beijing and Sydney. What does matter is that in each of these places you have had moments of realization, recognition or understanding. You carry home ideas and attitudes that you did not have before. You have learned something, and you are changed.

Such moments are particularly likely to occur for frugal travelers. Because they travel independently, with no intermediary between them and the culture they are visiting, they will have much first-hand interaction with local people. The more intense the experience, the more memorable and potentially life-changing. Frugal travel is more difficult—and yet often, I submit, more rewarding than mainstream travel.

Frugal travelers stretch their travel dollars farther and can get to a lot of places. They expect to work hard and even experience some discomfort. Hard work and discomfort are not in general, considered marketable. Selling the idea of travel requiring effort, challenge and stress is not easy. Thus, frugal travelers are a unique and special bunch. You must have a passion for travel if you intend to go this way—and this sets you apart.

This is a book for the passionate among you. You are willing to accept the possible hardships and difficulties of frugal travel in order to visit some of the world's most fascinating places— places you believe you might not otherwise have the resources to visit. You are willing to go as my husband George and I have gone, staying in hotels that will never be written up in *Travel Holiday.* Places like the spartan little hostel in Chiloe, Chile, which cost $5.60 a night (for a private room for two) and provides the widow proprietor with a small livelihood. Or the spare bedroom of a Portuguese couple who invited us to watch TV with them in their tiny living room. Or the sunny, upstairs room with a view of the Aegean to which we were led by a small boy when we got off the ferry on the Greek island of Paros. Or one of our favorites—the cavernous Number Two Guesthouse in the Chinese town of Dali, when the hot water in the concrete shower came on only between 5 and 7 p.m.

The mattresses in these places may have been thin and

3

saggy. Goats may have been bleating outside the window. It may have been a long and even dusty walk to town. But we were there! We got to see the bright blue and yellow fishing boats moored in Chiloe's harbors, stroll the beaches of the south coast of Portugal, photograph the vivid geraniums growing in olive oil tins along the cobblestone streets of the Greek islands, and marvel at a walled Chinese city where people wore blue Mao jackets and sold tobacco in bundles on the sidewalks.

We own these experiences. They are riches stashed away in the memory bank to be drawn out and enjoyed at will. Yours are awaiting you. I'll tell you everything I've learned about how to stake claim to them.

NOTE: Where money is mentioned in this book, it refers to United States dollars unless noted otherwise in the text.

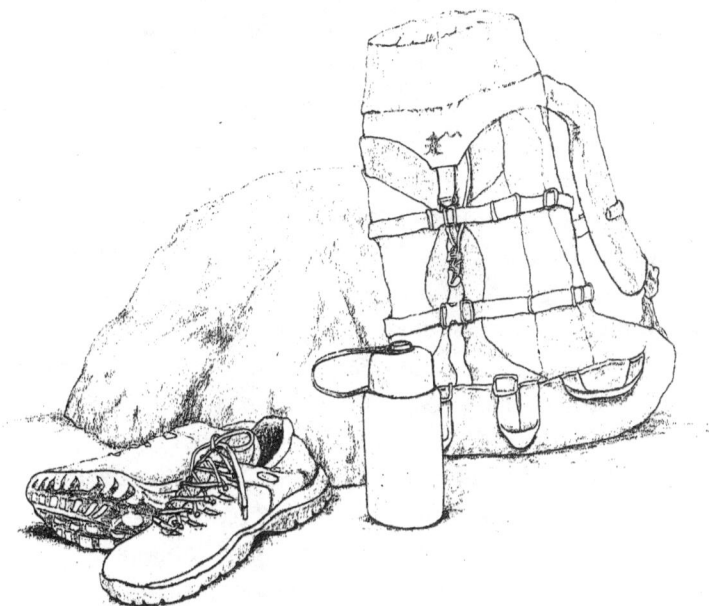

Chapter One

IS FRUGAL TRAVEL FOR YOU?

How frugal do you want to be? There are degrees of frugality. Some people are determined to get by on a rock-bottom budget; others are simply interested in moderate cost containment. Those whose dream is to travel in the world's more expensive countries will have to be satisfied with the latter. The tips in this book will help achieve cost savings in any country, but you will have to work hard to achieve bargains in the more highly developed places.

There are basically two kinds of countries in which to travel. The kind you choose has a lot to do with how much you'll have to spend. Developing countries where there is no car-owning middle class of any significant size, have cheap public transportation readily available. More developed places, such as the United States, have fewer public transportation options and they are often fairly costly.

When you bring up the subject of foreign travel, most Americans think of Europe first. They want to see Paris, visit London. Many Americans have ancestral roots in Europe, so it is no wonder they are curious about their countries of origin. However, if you are an ambitious traveler and want to maximize the number of countries you can visit in a lifetime of venturing forth, you may be drawn to less developed places,where costs are low.

I have a friend who just spent a winter in London with her professorial husband who was on sabbatical doing literary research. "Don't you ever go to any civilized countries?" she asked me when she learned we were making travel plans again.

We would like to spend some weeks going to the theater in London and eating Yorkshire pudding, but for the cost of two months in London we could probably spend six months in Asia.

I once sat next to a man on an airplane who asked me where I'd been. Bursting with enthusiasm about a just-completed visit to Bolivia, I started to describe our trip. But as soon as I said "Bolivia," he shook his *Wall Street Journal* dismissively. "I don't understand why anyone would want to go to a place like that and look at all the poverty," he said. That was the end of our conversation.

His response, like that of my friend who thought we ought to go to London, is not uncommon. Whenever we talk about our low-cost globetrotting to underdeveloped places, some peoples' eyes glaze over and it's clear they really don't want to hear another word about countries where people still carry water.

For George and me, these stark contrasts are what is captivating about less-developed places. It's like taking a trip in a time capsule back to what our own country was like two or three generations ago. These places are being yanked inevitably toward a global, uniform culture, so we are lucky to have the chance to see them while their uniqueness remains apparent, and some almost completely intact.

Those intrigued by this kind of travel press on with many questions, most of which are addressed in this book. One of the most frequently asked questions demonstrates the need for more books like this one to encourage independent travel.

"Did you have guides?" we are asked, as if to suggest that the world is such a forbidding place we could not possibly have made our way to and around such exotic destinations as Asia and South America without hired help leading the way.

"Were there snakes?" is another commonly asked (rather odd) question. We're not sure how to analyze that one, but when it is posed we try to be reassuring. We say that we did not encounter many snakes, but we do feel compelled to mention that snake charmers with cobras are a common sight in India, and we did have a memorable experience in the jungles of Thailand when a long, skinny snake did a little dance in front of us before it slithered off.

The most common question of all is impossible to answer. Everyone wants to know which country among those we've visited we liked the best. We say we can't pick a favorite because countries offer such a variety of experiences that we loved each one for something different, and would find it difficult to rank one above the other. How do you compare, for instance, trekking in Nepal among Himalayan snow peaks with gazing at fascinating pre-Columbian gold artifacts in a Lima museum? Or how do you rank photographing colorfully dressed South American Indians selling garbage sacks full of coca leaves in a marketplace against sitting with local villagers in a Buddhist *gompa* in Ladakh where masked dancers perform ancient rituals?

Every country offers different challenges and a different set of cultural norms to which the frugal traveler must respond. We have discovered that what we remember and love about a place are not only the spectacularly beautiful sights and intellectually stimulating moments, but also those times when we weren't so sure we really wanted to be there at all.

Which brings us to the crux of what sets frugal travel apart, particularly frugal travel to less-developed countries. The challenges and the close encounters with cultural differences are what make it interesting. It's not only seeing the sights, it's the

7

experiences you've gone through to get there. Frugal travelers are generally not traveling in an air-conditioned tour bus, a taxi or a rented car. They are taking local transportation, riding buses, trains, bicycle rickshaws or even ox carts. They are staying with local people, not in expensive, world-class hotels for foreigners. These tastes of reality may be a bit sharp, but they are the tastes travelers remember and enjoy telling about when they get home.

Here's an example. We settled into a small $10 a night hotel called the Rizwan in Srinagar, Kashmir, India. The Muslim men who ran the place were curious to a fault, even barging into our room without knocking. The door locked from the outside only, with a padlock, so we took to barricading the inside. That didn't stop one brash fellow who climbed onto the balcony outside our room and poked his head in the window. "Can you tell me please, what is the time?" he said.

These hotel keepers were fascinated by my Western-woman behavior. I went out wearing modest (I thought) knee-length shorts, without my husband, and rode my bicycle all over town. No Muslim women did any of these things. When I'd come back, they'd pester me with questions. Where had I been? What was I doing? I found their prying annoying, but tried to remain gracious. One day they got up the nerve to ask what was really on their minds. "How many sons do you have?" they wanted to know. I didn't give them the satisfaction of revealing that I had produced "only" two daughters.

Here's another example of memorable discomfort. In Katmandu, we signed up for a locally organized tour of the country's national wild animal park called Chitwan. The transportation was by local bus to the town nearest the park where we were to be met and taken to a lodge. The vehicle met us all right—it was an ox cart pulled by two water buffalo yoked together with one of those devices you see in museums in the U.S. It was driven by a small boy. The cart lurched along a dirt track for miles. We could have walked faster, but at least we weren't carrying our backpacks. It was totally dark when we forded a river. As our animals struggled to pull us through the current, we felt like pioneers crossing some

8

river in Kansas. I could only think that this was one of the most amazing evenings of my life. I will never need to go to a theme park to get a tangible sense of my country's past.

How Gutsy Are You?

One of the most difficult tasks of frugal travel for me is overcoming shyness or embarrassment in order to get what I need. No tour guide is taking care of me. I get as much information as I can from the books I have or the English speakers I encounter. However, at some point I am going to have to ask for help from someone who does not speak my language. Maybe because words are so important to me, I hate being inarticulate, ungrammatical, or, worst of all, completely unintelligible. Asking questions armed only with a phrase book or a rudimentary understanding of a foreign tongue means you are going to appear inarticulate. There's no escaping it.

Frugal travelers are made, not born, but if you don't have, or are unwilling to develop, the inner toughness it takes to risk looking silly, you are going to have an impossible time. Accepting this condition clears one of the major hurdles along the path to successful frugal travel.

An American physician told a friend of mine he would never go back to Paris because, during his one visit, the waiters in restaurants made him feel stupid. His French was poor, or maybe he knew none at all. In any case, they snickered about his attempts to order a meal, ruining his appetite for travel as well as for dinner.

The French, of course, are often criticized for snobbery about their language, but no matter where you travel you are going to risk being giggled at by service personnel because every one of them can speak Swahili, Urdu, Russian or Italian better than you. The idea is not to worry about it and remember the mission. You need to get fed, sheltered, or find out what time the bus leaves, and that is *all* that matters. Who cares if you sound like an idiot? If you can muster the courage to laugh at yourself along with those who are laughing at you, most foreigners will forgive you your inarticulateness and admire your guts. Not that you care, remember. You'll never see them again.

I can talk about it in the abstract and sound convincing, but in reality I struggle with this challenge every time I leave the country for a non-English-speaking destination. One memorably terrible moment occurred on a bus in China.

We were traveling on a local conveyance from Kunming to Dali, a day-long trip over poor roads. I made the mistake of having two cups of coffee at a hotel restaurant before we left at 8 a.m. By 10 a.m., I was in desperate need of a rest stop. I kept assuming everyone else was too, and the driver would soon pull over at some place with facilities.

Maybe all the Chinese on the bus knew better than to drink anything before a bus trip; maybe they had genetically copious bladders; maybe they drank herbal tea that caused the retention of bodily fluids. For some reason known only to him, the driver did not stop. By 11 a.m., I began to think he would not pull over before lunch. I knew I would never make it.

Finally, I gathered enough courage to ask for help. Clutching the phrase book I had just studied, I made my way to the front of the crowded bus. "Set swa," I said carefully to the driver in my best attempt at saying the word for toilet. He glanced over his shoulder at me blankly. "Set swa," I said, louder, and with a bit of a plaintive note. I heard a few titters from the people nearby. He looked at me again, more searchingly. Then he nodded.

I went back to my seat. Did he understand? Would he stop? I sat and squirmed—much to George's amusement. For some cosmically unfair reason, George wasn't in a similarly miserable state. I hated him.

Finally, we came to a small village and the driver pulled over and stopped the bus. I sprang for the door, but then hesitated, confused. I saw nothing that looked like a restroom. Then I noticed a tumble-down shack just off the road. Could it be? Yes! Inside were two planks over an unsavory hole in the ground. I've never in my life been so glad to see something approximating an outhouse.

10

Could You Love Developing-Country Frugal Travel?

Looking back on it, there was a moment when George and I should have realized we'd become confirmed under-developed-country frugal travelers. It was the time we gave up a free night at the luxurious Hilton International in Bangkok in order to stay in a rundown center-city hotel and spend $10 for the privilege.

We were on a whirlwind around-the-world TWA frequent flyer award trip. We had only four nights in Bangkok, and two of them, as a bonus from the airline, were to be at this fancy hotel. It was located several miles from the heart of the city and surrounded by acres of tropical gardens, pools, stone bridges and paths. It was heavenly, but we felt cloistered. Out there was a teeming, vibrant city, and we were not part of it. After one admittedly splendid night, we packed up the contents of the fruit bowl and checked out.

We were glad we did. We rode the river taxis with orange-robed Buddhist monks and small uniformed school children, dripped juice all over our clothes as we munched sweet pineapple on a stick, gasped at the traffic, haggled with *tuk-tuk* drivers over fares, choked on fiery street food, festooned ourselves with orchid necklaces, and bargained for a kilo of ground white pepper at the bustling Chinatown market. We ambled wearily back to our hotel at night where paint was peeling in the halls and a bare lightbulb swung from a cord in our room.

Sequestered at the Hilton, surrounded by beauty that purported to represent Thailand but showed us only a manicured facade, we would have felt deprived of discovering the real beauty down in the streets.

When given a choice, frugal travelers take encounter over luxury. Luxury is available anywhere. Only Bangkok can give you Bangkok.

We are convinced there are many potential frugal, independent travelers who haven't mustered the experience, confidence or courage to break out from more traditional travel. We met one such man in China.

We had just finished eating dinner on a street in Xian called

Heping Lu.

On summer nights Heping Lu becomes an outdoor bistro. Lights are strung from trees, vendors set up tables and portable kitchens, and enticing aromas fill the air. We found steamed buns filled with a savory meat, crisp greens in a tangy sauce, and broiled tidbits of something on bamboo skewers. A multi-generational family motioned us to share their table. The baby cried at the sight of George's beard, and the grandfather offered us beer in cracked mugs. We could not communicate, but there was smiling and nodding all around.

A fancy tour bus, much larger and more elegant than any ordinary Chinese bus, pulled up to a restaurant at one end of Heping Lu as we strolled in that direction toward a watermelon stand for dessert. A group of Westerners filed out of the restaurant and onto the bus. A man broke away from the line and came over to us, asking if we were Americans. He was from Minnesota.

"Did you eat here on the street?" he asked.

"Oh, yes," we told him, interrupting each other in our enthusiasm about the food, the people, the chefs who stirred their woks with such drama, and how cheap it was.

His meal, he said, was bland and probably expensive, though he didn't know for sure since he'd paid for the whole trip in a lump sum.

"Are you here on your own?"

We told him a little about our independent month in China— its challenges and charms. Then the bus rumbled to life and someone beckoned to him to get on board. He wanted to stay and talk, but his time in China, while it was costing him dearly, was not his own.

"Have a great trip," he said as he turned away. "I wish I were going with you."

How Sturdy Are You?

Finally, it is necessary to take a look at your physical as well as your mental profile . Frugal independent travelers can be called FITs for short—and with good reason. Besides being mentally prepared for the challenges involved with this kind of travel, you must also be physically fit and able.

Is this book relevant for senior citizens as well as for those in mid-life or youth? It's one thing for someone in their 20s or 40s to go off confidently to remote and primitive places in the world, but does it make sense to suggest that 70- or 80-year-olds do the same?

It would be ageist to suggest that someone should be excluded from becoming a FIT because of years alone. Multitudes of 20-year-olds could not cut it as frugal travelers. You have to have the curiosity, desire and passion to see the world. You need the determination to put up with the difficulties, and you must have or develop the chutzpa to ask your way, while allowing any snickering roll off your back. Last, and perhaps least, you have to have the physical stamina and general good health to endure the stress and strain of moving about from town to town and room to room, hauling your gear around, walking a lot, eating strange food, and in general adapting to an unsettled existence. Few seniors are willing to undertake the adventure of frugal independent travel but those who are willing may certainly be able.

We met a German couple who were 65 and trekking on their own in Nepal. They had one porter helping them and they were keeping up with multitudes of trekkers on the Annapurna Circuit —all of whom were younger than they. They were inspiring, not to mention popular. Everyone there knew their names and asked how they were faring whenever they met up. The couple crossed the 18,000-foot Thorong La pass without a problem when several young travelers had to give up and turn back due to altitude sickness. Oddly enough, older folks routinely have less trouble with altitude-related illness than do younger people.

I recently heard a story about a pair of white-haired backpackers in Canyonlands National Park near Moab, Utah. Someone who encountered them in the harsh and beautiful desert asked their ages. They were in their 90s. When questioned about how they could possibly manage at such an age, they said they had just never stopped exerting their bodies in this strenuous way.

13

We met a 57-year-old Canadian on a Mexican bus one February. He had taken early retirement from teaching to travel, and was on a journey with his 28-year-old son. He hoped for a long life, he said, having just read an article about achieving longevity in Omni magazine. The article said a person needed good social support, a purpose (something worthwhile to do), and, finally, he or she must be awestruck about life.

We laughed together about this last characteristic, for we understood without saying this was one of the reasons we were all on that bus together. Frugal travelers of all ages are awestruck about the world and their existence in it.

Chapter Two
HOW TO GET STARTED

In frugal travel, advance planning means the difference between success and failure. However, there is a difference between advance planning and setting up a rigid itinerary. Frugal travelers must do a lot of the former and strictly avoid the latter.

Frugal travel is flexible travel. FITs (frugal independent travelers) cultivate serendipity. For example, a person in the room down the hall has just told you about a great, cheap little inn in a town you weren't even planning to visit. The bus doesn't make the trip until Wednesday, but that's okay—you can work it out. Frugal travelers expect the unexpected and take advantage of what falls in their laps.

Before you leave home gather as much information as you can about your destination. Happy frugal travelers are informed.

A friend called me for advice. "I have collected an insurance settlement," she said, "I feel like jumping on a plane and going somewhere wonderful. Greece maybe. I'll just come back when I run out of money. What do you think?"

Such an impulse is compelling. I hated to dampen her enthusiasm, but I advised her to slow down and spend some time on analysis and research. Is this the best time to be in Greece? How much money can you afford to spend? How much does it cost there? Is it considered a safe destination by the U.S. State Department? How much time do you have? What restrictions do you have to meet to get the best airfare? Do you want to go alone or with a friend? Are you compatible? Can you travel within the country more cheaply if you buy some air, bus or train tickets in the U.S. before you go? There are dozens of such questions that need to be addressed. Take the time to find the answers before you go to insure a satisfying trip with optimum cost-containment.

Is it Safe?

The U.S. Government will make no guarantee about your welfare, but they will let you know which countries the state department considers unsafe for Americans to visit—at this time. Call their hotline (202-647-5225 or -5226), punch in the number asking for a list of countries on the warning list. Enter a few letters to hear a full report on any country on the list. At the time of this writing there were twenty-three—most of them in Africa.

In Nigeria, for example, the message says that currently uniformed men commonly "shake down" foreigners, robbing them of their valuables. In addition, there is violent crime. The air fleet is obsolete and poorly maintained, and business scams are common. You also learn the number of the embassy so if you want to talk about getting a visa anyway, you can do so. The music and nightlife are supposed to be terrific. Only don't take much money. And keep in mind, if you go into Nigeria without a visa, they can prevent you from leaving.

Going Alone

I have not taken any major trips alone. I think I could, but I love having a travel-buddy with whom to share the experiences. However, people who are eager to travel need not stay home for want of a companion. Several books address the issues associated with solo travel. One I've found helpful is *A Foxy Old Woman's Guide to Traveling Alone,* by Jay Ben-Lesser. She gives a compact bundle of suggestions on safety and satisfaction for solo women travelers. Other books and newsletters are listed in the appendix and book list.

Traveling Companions

If your preference is to go with another person, or if you are hooked up with a mate who wants to go too, clarify some issues before your departure.

How bio-synchronous are you? If you need the same amount of sleep, have similar amounts of energy, and get hungry at about the same time, you're in luck. Your traveling compatibility factor should be high. Such synchronicity is rare, so be prepared to cope with differences by compromising and working out ways both persons' needs can be accommodated.

What about interests? George hates shopping, so when I want to browse, he volunteers to take a nap. We often spend either the morning or the afternoon apart, George at a coin museum, or tracing the history of science and industry while I look at folk or fine art. Separations to pursue individual interests relieve some of the tension that can easily develop with the forced togetherness of travel. Besides, it gives us material to talk about over dinner.

An important issue for a frugal traveling pair is the degree of frugality each is hoping to achieve. What are each person's requirements in terms of comfort levels? I've heard of more than one trip where companions have split up mid-adventure because they were incompatible in this basic area. One person may think an $80-a-night hotel room in a European city is a bargain, while the other assumed they would spend far less by staying in hostels or working-class neighborhood pensions. One may have been expecting to have a sit-down restaurant meal three times a day, while the other thought they would put together breakfast and lunch from open air markets or street vendors. One may have expected hotel rooms with private bathrooms. The other may be willing to accept more communal arrangements. Hashing out a budget together is one way you will be sure to raise these issues. Creating a budget is the most crucial advanced planning FITs must undertake. (See the Appendix for information on the *Travel Companion Exchange*.)

Deciding on a Budget

You may be wondering how you can come up with a budget before you even decide what countries you're going to visit. The answer is that your budget may determine where you *can* spend time. Say you plan on traveling for a month and you have $50 a day to spend for the two of you after you've covered airfare. With this budget, you can afford some countries and some you cannot.

This is the point when you get down to the nitty gritty. How

17

are you willing to live? In Ecuador, George met a couple of young Australians (a country with the world's most dedicated travelers, we've come to believe), who were planning to travel for two years in South America on $5 a day. They lived in a tent, cooked all their meals on a backpacking stove, and hitchhiked. They set up this austere budget in order to maximize the duration of their trip. Few frugal travelers are this dedicated. However, these two showed the rest of us what is possible.

In a more moderate vein, in many countries, including several in South America, a couple can sleep in hotels, eat in restaurants and take public transportation for an average of $30 to $50 a day. Between $50 and $100 a day for two provides an upscale lifestyle in most less-developed countries. In western Europe, however, you will have to spend more unless you are willing to camp or stay in hostels.

Once you have come up with the amount you can spend, you are one step closer to being ready to match your resources to specific destinations.

Deciding on the Length of Your Trip
A common adage says travelers should bring twice the money and half the clothes they'd planned to bring. For frugal travelers, the idea has a different spin. You can bring half the money of typical tourists, but be prepared to spend twice the time.

Frugal travel requires an investment of time every day simply to take care of basic needs. Finding food, shelter and transportation independently in a strange place where you may not even speak the language can be a daunting task. If you're prepared, you'll have a guidebook or two to help—but you are still on your own.

A traveler on a tour, or the independent tourist with a fat wallet, spends no time in this way. They or their agents have already reserved rooms, buses or taxis to take them to see the sights, and they eat at hotels or nearby restaurants with three to five stars.

Frugal travelers rarely make hotel reservations. Small, family-

18

owned establishments don't appear in travel agents' computers, may not be listed in guidebooks, and seldom have fax machines. (We've stayed in many that don't even have electricity.)

Although an advance reservation for the first night or so in a destination country offers reassurance, most of the time frugal travelers try to arrive in a new town or city early enough in the day to hunt up a place to stay, figure out the public transportation, and find simple restaurants catering to locals. With these tasks before them, it is not possible for FITs to "do" a city in one day and then zoom off to another. They must allow a day in every new place to get settled and oriented. Then they can visit the sights, browse the markets, hike the hills, or whatever it is they came there to do.

It is this time requirement that keeps many people from even considering independent frugal travel as an option. They are not willing or able to invest the kind of time needed to succeed. Yet it is precisely this time requirement that makes frugal travel not only less expensive but also more interesting than tours or high-budget travel. Being forced to hunt up small hotels, local restaurants and bus stations puts you elbow-to-elbow with the native citizenry. Opportunities for cultural observation and comparison abound.

Finding More Time for Travel

Americans, on average, have less vacation time than citizens of fourteen other developed countries. This is an issue I believe we, as a society, need to examine—but in the meantime, how can Americans take extended trips? Simple. You have to rearrange your priorities.

George and I have organized our lives around increasing the opportunities to do what we love. We save money by living frugally—driving old cars, cooking from scratch and never carrying a balance on our credit card. Ten years ago we took leaves of absence from our jobs, rented out the house to cover the mortgage, and traveled for a year. We spent less than if we'd stayed at home—about $15,000. We continued to save after that, working toward early retirement, which we achieved at age 55. Now we *really* have time to travel.

During our year of learning to be FITs, the importance of having sufficient time to travel in this manner was apparent to us in every country we visited. I kept a journal, and here's how we spent the day we arrived in Xian, China.

A Day in China

We landed in Xian on a plane from Chongqing about 10 a.m. An airport bus went to the town. We followed the crowd and got on. It delivered us all to the ticket office of the airline. This was lucky, since the only way to make reservations to fly somewhere else was to appear in person in the city from which you hoped to depart. No telephone reservation system was available. It took half an hour.

Once we had our tickets to leave a few days hence, we set off to find a hotel room. Two hotels were permitted to house foreigners at the time. Our guidebook gave us their names and the bus numbers that would get us there. We stood at the bus stop and watched in amazement as people pushed and shoved their way onto the next crowded bus that stopped.

We learned fast, and jammed ourselves into the bus headed toward the Victory Hotel. We had some height advantage over most Chinese, which enabled us to keep track of each other on the bus. The fare for a long ride was 3/4 of a cent each.

At the hotel, we got a room, settled in, then rented bicycles to find a place to eat. We were happy to come across a place a few blocks away called The Small World that catered to the hotel guests. After lunch we had to change money, locate the tourist office in order to buy a good map of the city, and buy tickets for a mini-bus tour the next day to see the famous clay warriors unearthed in Xian. Finally, we were ready to take a spin on our bikes to see something of the beautiful, walled, ancient city of Xian, but we were too tired. Besides, we had to be back at our hotel for scheduled showers—hot water was on in the cavernous communal (single sex) baths from 5 p.m. to 7 p.m. only.

20

It had been a challenging day, but our confidence was growing. We were coping on our own in China and what an experience we were having.

Choosing a Country

Clip a currency exchange rate list out of a newspaper (the *Wall Street Journal* publishes one every weekday). With this in hand, seek out recent guidebooks for the countries that interest you. Now is a terrific time to be a frugal traveler. Many great guidebooks are available for every imaginable destination, so you can be well informed about what to expect. Several series stress independent, budget travel, including my favorite, the *Lonely Planet* guides. Others are the *Moon Travel Handbooks, Frommer, Let's Go, Berkeley Guides, Rough Guides,* and the handbooks for South and Central America, Mexico and Asia.

If your library doesn't have current volumes, bookstores do. Find one with a comfortable spot for leisurely study. There's no point in buying a guide until you've decided where you are going. Nor should you buy until you are sure you are getting the most recent title to be published before your departure. New versions come out every couple of years and information changes considerably during that length of time.

Sometimes you can't get a book that is new enough to suit you. Research for a book called *Indonesia 2000* was probably done in 1998. If you think you need really up to the minute information, you can probably find it on the Internet. Lonely Planet Publications, for example, updates their books online. Go to lonelyplanet.com, find your country and see what changes may be posted.

Many guidebooks will tell you what dollar value they place on an expensive, moderate and inexpensive hotel room. Others quote prices in the local currency. Use your exchange rate to determine the likely price at the moment. If you can't seem to find hotels listed at prices you can afford, you may have to give up on that paticular country and find one that costs less to visit.

NOTE: A good rule of thumb is to spend no more than half your daily allowance on a room—less if possible.

Don't let go of your dreams too easily, however. Look for some other options. In our experience it is often possible to find small, out-of-the-way, family-owned, moderately priced accommodations even in developed countries.

How can you find out if such places exist? Look in guidebooks for 800 numbers for tourist information. Call these countries' tourist offices and ask for information about low-cost accommodations.

George and I had almost given up on going to New Zealand because the guidebooks indicated that even rooms in the "inexpensive" category were beyond our budget. Luckily, a government publication from the U.S.-based tourist office informed us the country has many hostels open to anyone, not just students. These places had private rooms (bring your own bedding), were located in most towns and cities, and offered shared bathrooms and communal kitchens. The cost was 1/3 that of a regular hotel or motel room. We thought that sounded great, booked our flights and packed our bags. We spent an inexpensive month in New Zealand and plan to go back.

Staying in hostels in developed countries—hostels which, in many cases, have improved greatly from the days of huge dorm rooms full of bunk beds—is one of the easiest ways to make travel to such destinations affordable.

Another frugal way to go is camping. We first tried this in Puerto Rico. Resort hotels cost much more than we wanted to spend, and even smaller, family-owned inland places had nightly price tags above our budget for this trip. We dug around and discovered that the island has a number of government-run campgrounds. With a rental car, a tent and a few supplies, we spent two weeks exploring the island, sleeping in safe, fenced, beach-front accommodations every night for about $10. We got to know a few Puerto Rican boy scouts as well.

Encouraged by that experience, in 1997 we tackled one of the most popular and expensive resort destinations in the United States. We brought a cooler this time as a piece of luggage (filled with camping gear), we rented cars on three of Hawaii's most scenic islands and managed ocean-view living for an average of $2 a night at the many state and county campgrounds. Cooking our own meals helped, and even with a car our daily expenses were around $50 for two. In Hawaii.

Camping is also popular in Europe. While I camped my way through six countries 30 years ago, George and I have yet to try it together but we will.

More possibilities exist. Home exchanges work for some people, particularly if they have a house to swap in a desirable place in the United States. A stay of a month or more in one spot might be reasonably priced if you rent an apartment or house. There are books listing current rental agencies by country, and several home exchange organizations—check out the Appendix. Some countries have English language newspapers which advertise rooms, apartments or houses to rent. The *Tico Times* in Costa Rica is an example. Guidebooks often refer to such resources.

If your philosophy is compatible with the intentions of the international peace and friendship organization called Servas, you may be able to join and visit the homes of fellow members in destination countries. Membership is particularly strong in more developed places. See the Appendix for more details.

Weather and Climate

Don't make your final choice of countries to visit until you've studied up on seasonal details. Many tropical and subtropical countries have rainy periods you will probably want to avoid. In Costa Rica the rainy season is called "winter," but takes place during the summer months. In northern Australia, the "big wet" arrives in their summer—December, January and February. Other parts of Australia are delightful at that time of year, however. Know before you go.

Selecting Guidebooks

Guidebooks which offer more cultural commentary and history than practical information are nice to read before you go, but if space is limited, they are not the ones you'll want to carry with you. Since their information is less likely to be dated, read library copies of such books (*Insight Guides* is a good example of such a series) and save your money for buying the latest edition of the book you need to take along. Ask the bookstore to check on the scheduled date of publication for the newest edition and buy it, if possible.

Frugal travelers I've met save weight in their backpacks by tearing out sections of a larger book—such as the weighty *South American Handbook*—that apply to their destination. It seems a sacrilege to tear up a book, especially a new, expensive one, but it makes sense.

Another possibility is photocopying the most helpful pages of a book you own but would rather not carry.

Flying

Transcontinental transportation usually represents the largest single expense for FITs (unless, of course, you've been frugally collecting frequent flyer miles). Many Americans swear the travel agent they always deal with can get them the best price available. After all, she has it all right there on her computer. In our experience, it just ain't so.

Again, diligent research pays off in big savings. Much of the work has been done for us. Whole books have been written on the subject of how to get a low cost airplane ticket. One excellent example is *Insider Travel Secrets* (Best Fares, Inc. 1997), by Tom Parsons.

In a nutshell, here are my tips.

1. *Air Courier.* Some people swear by the savings that come with being an air courier. You pay nothing or, more often, a reduced fare to give your luggage allotment to a company that wants to transport something quickly to another country. Books have been written on the subject (see Appendix), but the disadvan-

24

tages may put you off. You can't easily travel with a companion, you are limited to one carry-on bag in most cases, and your schedule is also not your own. But check it out if the cost of getting there is a big obstacle for you.

2. *Direct Calls to Airlines.* These days you can make direct calls on toll-free numbers to numerous domestic and international airlines. Begin your inquiries several months in advance, if possible. Make a list of the airlines that serve your destinations (this information is often in guidebooks) and the dates you hope to travel. Then call each airline, tell them you are looking for the best possible price, and that you are flexible about the days of the week you can travel, the time of day, and even the destination. For example, it may not seriously matter to you if you land in Athens or Frankfurt on a trip to Europe if one city turns out to cost much less than the other. If they quote you a price, and you've had a better offer, tell them so. I have actually had airline personnel negotiate with me over fares.

Write down everything. If you find something you like, they will ask if they can book the seats for you. Don't do it unless you know the details. How soon, for example, do you have to follow the reservation with a credit card payment? Is the ticket fully refundable? If not, what are the conditions? Are the dates changeable? At what cost? What other restrictions are there? Be sure to get the reservation number so you can call back to purchase or cancel.

3. *Ticket Discounters.* Buy a copy of the Sunday paper from your departure airport city as well as from the major international airport nearest you, such as New York, Miami or Los Angeles. In the travel section there are always ads by ticket brokers selling discounted seats to international (as well as domestic) destinations. In our experience these are legitimate and reliable businesses, but take your time making a decision and giving out your credit card number. Make sure you have comparison information, and are comfortable with your choice. The broker may pressure you into buying quickly ("Only a few seats are left at that price") but take your time. Cheap seats are not all that scarce.

Discounters buy their tickets from ticket consolidators, who buy blocks of unsold seats from commercial airlines and charters. Call or visit the web sites of several with the itinerary you have in mind. Compare with your earlier deals. Again, have them spell out the cancellation, refund and modification stipulations before you buy.

4. *Don't Buy Frequent Flyer Awards.* Beware of buying frequent flyer award tickets from individuals or businesses in the classified ads. Some of these tickets may be legitimately transferred or sold, but it is usually against airline policy. If you buy such a ticket, the airline can deny you the use of the ticket when you arrive for boarding. Check with the airline before you buy.

5. *No Cheap Seats?* If you cannot find an inexpensive ticket, reserve a seat that you can afford, making sure the ticket is fully refundable. Then keep looking for a discounted ticket. Airlines often run last-minute specials or free up another block of cheaper seats as departure date draws near and they have empty seats.

6. *Internet Ticket Purchases.* Buying international airplane tickets on the Internet is a new and still unsettled method of obtaining discounted fares. Airlines have their own web sites, and industry observers predict Internet fare wars will become standard operating procedure. *USA Today* recently reported that airlines watch each others' on-line offers and subsequently match or better them. Such competition has been giving consumers 20 to 30 percent discounts on domestic flights. How much of this will spill over to international routes remains to be seen. The newspaper suggests checking with Tom Parsons, editor of *Best Fares* magazine.He tracks fare deals on his website, www.bestfares.com.

Also, check www.priceline.com, a web site where you can make an offer on a ticket, both domestic and international, and see if your bid is accepted. The catch is, while you can request a day of departure and return, you have no say in what time these flights go, and you can't choose the airline.

Internet air travel purchases are in a state of flux. You can keep up to date on what's available by reading the travel section of your Sunday newspaper or picking up copies of travel related magazines such as, *Consumer Reports Travel Letter* and *Best Fares.*

7. **Last Minute Travel.** We haven't tried this, but it is becoming common practice for airlines to list unsold seats at steep discounts on the Internet just days before flights. If you have the flexibility and nerve, this could be a way to get out of the country at a rock bottom price. Check with the airlines that serve your destination for the necessary e-mail addresses. Sometimes, you can ask them to send you a weekly update.

Also, investigate travel organizations that keep track of last minute deals on cruises, tours and simple international flights. You keep your bags packed and check with the hot lines of such groups. In most cases you must pay an annual membership fee to use their services. A list of last-minute travel organizations is in the Appendix.

8. **Frequent Flyer Awards.** If you have sufficient miles to obtain one or two round trip tickets to a country that interests you, make your reservations well in advance—up to a year is permitted in most cases. The airlines are not eager to give away seats on their best routes so they restrict the number of free seats available. Try a variety of dates if the one you want is full, then ask to be wait-listed since reservations are often made and later canceled.

Remember, the number of points required to obtain a free ticket will sometimes vary with the time of year. Fewer are required for off-season travel. Be aware of blackout dates when *no* frequent flyer seats are available.

9. **Open Jaws.** After doing your airfare research (and before actually buying a ticket), you may decide to add or subtract from the list of countries you were planning to visit. George and I discovered, when we set up our frequent flyer tickets to and from South America, we could obtain an "open jaw" ticket that would allow us to come home from another city, different from the one we flew into, for the same round trip ticket cost. We decided to start in Santiago and fly home from Lima . . . traveling between the two cities overland through several countries for four months.

10. *Advance Purchases for Domestic Travel.* Many countries offer discounted travel within their borders to visitors who purchase vouchers while still at home. Look for details in guidebooks—but study the offers carefully. While intra-Argentinian flights may be a bargain, are you sure you want to fly between cities? Maybe you have time, and it would be cheaper, to take a bus. Often these deals are too restrictive for the frugal traveler, requiring you to do all your travel within three weeks when you were planning to stay three months. However, they are worth examination.

Take a Practice Trip or Two

If you are inexperienced at international independent travel, you may want to take a practice trip as part of your preparation for a longer trip. Pick a moderately developed country—somewhere between developed and developing, such as Greece or Portugal—and spend a couple of weeks there making your own way. Like any skill, the more you do it, the easier it gets.

If you aren't sure how to categorize a country, I'll give you some guidelines. (Look at individual guidebooks if you want more exact information on costs.) North America, including Canada and the United States, as well as Western Europe, Australia, New Zealand and Japan are clearly the world's most developed areas. Most of Asia, Eastern Europe, Africa (with the exception of Israel and South Africa), South and Central America, and Mexico would be considered developing, by varying degrees. Argentina, Chile and Mexico, for example, have more of a middle class than do Bolivia, Ecuador and Guatemala.

George and I are grateful we spent four months in South America before we traveled to Asia. Even though both are developing areas, South America was good training for coping with the enormously different cultures of India, China and Thailand.

The shock of India was significant. We brazenly arrived in Delhi without hotel reservations at 10 p.m., hoping for a bargain. A person at the traveler's information desk helped us get a cheap room, and also directed us to the airport bus that would get us to the hotel.

It was June, and sleeping bodies littered the floor of the airport—people taking advantage of the air conditioning. Along the streets, on the way to town, the sidewalks were blocked with beds—again full of people trying to beat the heat. We weren't at all sure our bus driver knew where we wanted to get off, but finally he did gesture us to disembark, and pointed vaguely off into the darkness. We gingerly stepped over and around sleeping people as we made our way toward the small neon sign of our hotel. We had to hammer on the door for a long while before the attendant unlocked the door and let us in. We felt very far from home.

Time is Money

Planning your own international FIT trip takes an enormous amount of time and effort, but the investment will pay great returns, both short and long term. In the short term you will be able to make a trip for hundreds or even thousands of dollars less than someone who hires others to do their planning and arranging for them; and you may even find the process fun and satisfying once you get caught up in it. In the long term, once you are home again you will have priceless memories to share and enjoy the rest of your life. What better payoff could there be?

Chapter Three

WHAT TO TAKE, AND HOW TO CARRY IT

Where you are going and how you plan to get around once you arrive, determines how much and what kind of stuff you'll need to bring—and how you are going to carry it. As mentioned earlier, developing counties tend to have extensive, inexpensive public transportation. Utilizing 3/4-cent bus rides is certainly one way to keep costs down.

If you are traveling to a developing country or countries, or if you are visiting developed countries but plan to depend on public transportation, you will fall into one luggage category, whereas if you are planning to rent, buy or lease a car, you are in another. If your itinerary (loose and flexible though it is) includes countries where you expect to do some of both kinds of travel, things get more complicated, but are still manageable.

We'll assume you've decided you want to see more of the world for less; you are going to visit developing countries. Therefore, you are going to want to travel light. Every how-to travel book written advises readers to pack light. Here's how.

Backpacks: The Luggage of Choice

Frugal travelers already familiar with inexpensive international travel, or those who have enjoyed recreational backpacking in our country's mountains and forests, may not find this a startling idea. However, for some urban, sport-utility vehicle driving, middle-aged Americans, the idea of hoisting on a backpack and looking like a graying hippie might seem a bit of a stretch. Trust me—in this situation, you have no other choice.

I was a most reluctant backpacker on the first trip we tried this approach. I was 47, and it seemed to me backpacking travelers were mostly European youths in need of a bath and a haircut. I pictured myself making this year-long trip wearing a crisp cotton skirt and jacket, a classy leather garment bag slung easily over my shoulder. My hair would be shiny, with a stylish cut. As it turned out, I wore black twill slacks with a cotton knit jacket. I carried a large pack strapped to my back, and a smaller one clasped to my front. My hair, if anyone could see me under my bags, was undoubtedly limp.

This sounds grimmer than it was. My vague goal of looking fashionable was incompatible with the more practical imperatives of frugal travel. These require you to simplify, layer, and pack multi-functional clothes that can be washed in sinks, rolled up into tiny balls, and crammed mercilessly into any available cranny of your pack. More importantly, if you can't carry, with relative comfort, what you have brought along, you compromise your ability to travel frugally.

Backpacks are the answer for several reasons. They have a limited capacity. Even if you buy a large backpack (not recommended), you cannot put as much in it as you can in a suitcase or duffel bag. The cubic inches of your pack will force you to carefully curtail the amount of clothes you bring. The good news is you can get along with a lot less than you would ever have imagined possible.

Second, backpacks are designed to be carried on your back. Your back is much stronger than two dangling arms. Depending on your size and gender, you can support 25 to 45 or 50 pounds quite comfortably. FITs must be prepared to walk, sometimes for a healthy distance. The bus may not stop near your hotel; the buses may have quit for the night; the bus drivers may be on strike. With suitcases or duffels you are stuck. You have to hail a taxi, blowing the day's budget—or even the week's. With a backpack, you are mobile and self-sufficient.

Backpacks protect you in several ways from those who sometimes prey upon vulnerable travelers. Your hands are free to fish out passports, focus a camera, look for tickets and money, or

32

thumb through your guidebook for an address—all without having to set down a bag. A bag on a sidewalk or concourse is a tempting target for a hit-and-run thief. Backpacks also look like less attractive booty than more stylish bags, and may be passed over by those hoping for jewelry, electronics, or cash.

A delightful virtue of a backpack for a shopper like me is, ironically, it makes it possible to bring home a large quantity of great stuff. On international flights each person may check two bags: the first with a length, height and width dimension of about 62 inches, and the second of 55 (this varies, so call your airline). If you check only one backpack on your departing flight, you can carry a duffel (or buy a basket, like we did in India) to fill with goodies to bring home on your return flight.

In Peru, we stuffed a duffel with handknit alpaca wool sweaters. In Indonesia, where the shopping is legendary, we filled a duffle bag with batik fabric and resort wear and then packed a cardboard box with baskets, carvings and more batik.

Finally, a backpack is something of a badge. It signifies you are a member of an unorganized but frugal, friendly and congenial international club. Backpackers come in all ages from countries all over the world. Generally they are as well-scrubbed as anyone, and they are certainly the most independent and knowledgeable travelers you will meet. Hotels in various countries around the world beckon them with their names. Stay in downtown Sydney at Eva's Backpackers in a comfortable double room for under $30 a night.

When we arrived in South America on the first leg of our year-long trip, I learned that middle-aged backpackers were not uncommon. They are known, in Spanish, as *mochileros*—after the word *mochila,* meaning backpack. In developing countries, or any place where you must be able to carry everything you brought in order to move to your next destination, a backpack is the perfect FIT luggage. I have become an enthusiastic *mochilera.*

Choosing a Backpack

If you have any previous backpacking experience, meaning you've gone into the wilderness carrying everything you need to sustain life for several days and walked until you thought you might never walk again, you know how important it is to choose a backpack that fits you properly.

There are those who would sell you a "convertible pack." This is a piece of luggage that can be carried on your back with straps and a belt, or carried over your shoulder or in your hand like a soft-sided suitcase. There's even one with wheels that will trundle along like the popular drag-it-behind you bag. They all look rather slick, and may be a good choice for someone who has no intention of ever going on a wilderness trek, or even carrying a pack on her back for more than 500 feet.

My experience tells me you could be making an expensive mistake. These bags often open to a roomy, rectangular storage compartment which you will certainly overload. Worse, they are not likely to be well-designed for carrying on your back. I had one once and it was torture.

It's better to select a true camping backpack at an outdoor store where a knowledgeable staffer can fit you with a bag that's appropriate for your body. Such bags come in many sizes and have adjustments within sizes for a custom fit. They distribute the weight so it is supported by your shoulders, back and legs. Thus, a properly fitted pack will feel like an extension of your body—not like a millstone pulling you backwards.

Further complicating your decision, you will find two types of camping backpacks: internal and external frames. Internal frame packs may make more sense for airplane travel, since with the frame tucked inside you have no exposed structure to get broken, bent or caught on luggage conveyors. Also, they are more flexible than external frame packs, and you can more easily stuff them into overhead bus compartments, or under seats. They are easier to cover with a garbage bag if you should need to protect your gear from a monsoon on the roof of a Nepali bus or on the back of a Himalayan pack horse.

Pack capacity is measured in cubic inches and varies from about 3,000 to 6,000. Unless she is a real brute, a woman may not want to exceed 4,000 cubic inches of capacity. Most men probably won't want more than 5,000 cubic inches of capacity.

Many newly designed packs feature plentiful exterior pockets. While this is great for backpacking, for traveling it's a liability. Luggage handlers could easily open and steal whatever is in these pockets. Better to select a pack with large compartments which you can lock by fastening the zipper slides together with small brass key-locks from the hardware store. (Sometimes you can find several locks that will all work with the same key. Look for the same identifying number.)

A knife-wielding assailant can of course slit and pilfer locked backpacks, like any soft-sided luggage, but our bags have never been cut and the locks have protected the contents.

If you do get a pack with exterior pockets, leave them empty for the trip over so you will have room for mementos. Then, on the way back, put your worn out and dirty socks in those pockets. If they get stolen, you won't mind.

Packing: Distinguish Between Wants and Needs

Clothes I love to wear at home and *want* to take with me on long trips are the very clothes I know I have to leave behind. Jeans, 100% cotton shirts and silk blouses that don't wash in the sink or dry fast should stay at home in your closet. A boon to women travelers are the crushed, purposefully wrinkled cottons and silks. They are perfect for travel, as are cotton knits.

NOTE: TravelSmith and Magellan sell a line of wrinkle-free, easy wash and dry travel clothes. Their phone numbers and addresses are in the Appendix.

The most important things I've learned about packing for frugal travel are to take only separates that mix and match. Stick to one basic dark color, such as black, brown or navy that you can brighten up with two or three coordinating prints or plain colors.

Take items that have several functions and that you can layer. Take only what you know you love to wear, and take very little. I was not convinced I could spend four months in South America with only one boring black knit skirt for dress-up, but I did.

Clothes selection depends more on the climate of the destination and the activities you'll undertake than the length of the trip. You actually need the same basic core wardrobe whether you are traveling for two weeks or ten months. As it happens, you can bring more clothes on a short trip because you will not have to save room for survival gear. More about that later.

Here's a suggested core list—clothes that will go on any trip to any destination with moderate temperatures. Extremes of weather or activities will demand some additions or subtractions. The list can be modified to suit either gender, but it is aimed at women who, after all, tend to care more about this anyway.

- 2 pairs long pants. I take jeans only if I know I'm going to a country with coin laundries.
- 1 pair long shorts or culottes
- 1 pair exercise shorts
- 1 skirt, dark color
- Coordinating top for dressy occasion
- Another for casual. Both should go with your pants.
- 1 long sleeved button-up shirt for layering
- 2 or 3 T-shirts
- 1 sleeveless knit top
- 1 set of light cotton knit sweats for night clothes, "bathrobe," and exercise
- 1 wind/rain jacket, hooded
- 1 pair sturdy walking shoes
- 1 pair sandals (summer) or flats
- 1 pair flip-flops or water sandals (Tevas) for showers, beaches
- 1 swimsuit if needed
- 5 pair undies
- 2 bras plus athletic bra
- 4 or 5 pairs socks
- 2 pair pantyhose

- Hat: sun shading

For cold weather add:
- silk or knit long underwear
- wool socks
- wind/rain pants
- polar fleece pullover, jacket or cardigan
- gloves/mittens
- wool or fleece cap

For trekking, hiking or other outdoor adventuring add:
- 1 pair comfortable hiking boots
- hiking socks (liners plus heavier pair)
- other activity-specific gear (it is not easy to rent outdoor gear in many developing countries)

For very hot climates: substitute cool, airy cotton tops, shorts, pants or skirts. Keep them modest.

Don't despair about this meager list. It's much better to start out with what looks like a rock-bottom basic collection and add as you go. Inevitably you will see interesting items you would like to buy and wear as you travel. In fact, if you are traveling to a country such as Indonesia, India or Thailand, where inexpensive tropical clothing is sold on the sidewalks, you'll be happier if you bring almost nothing with you but your bathing suit and what you wear on the plane. All the other tourists in these places will be wearing comfortable cottons in bright local prints. That's the garb you'll want, too.

Did you notice my list focuses on comfort? I want to have the right thing to wear for any temperature I encounter—from a stuffy bus to a freezing ferry. I keep items to adjust my comfort level handy in a small day pack. Not everyone is this particular. George is not, and carries fewer clothes. He can get along on so little it boggles the mind.

Mochileros in Chile

Mochileros all have tales to tell that recall moments when they have been happy they had backpacks instead of conventional luggage (or tales of how they suffered with conventional luggage before they switched). We remember being happy to have our packs to use as seats when our only other choice was the hard floor of a jouncing truck in Bolivia. We were glad, too, we could throw them on top of buses, or stuff them into tuk-tuks in Asia. A night in Chile stands out in my memory.

Our usual routine in Chile had been to check our packs at the bus station in a little office called a *custodial* while we hunted up a hotel. We rarely agreed right away on a place to stay. George wanted economy and a short distance to carry his pack. I was willing to pay more and walk farther if I could find a place with a little charm. Ultimately, we'd compromise, selecting something we could both accept.

In the icy little town of Coyhaique, far south along Chile's island-studded coast, we could not exercise our little routine. We pulled in well after dark, and the bus drove off as soon as we were all unloaded. The bus station was closed, and the local folks quickly scattered. We would have considered splurging on a taxi, if one were to be found, but the street was dark and deserted, apparently at the edge of town. Another pair of travelers, a Belgian couple, stood with us, looking just as uncertain. It began to rain.

We set off down the road toward lights we thought must be the town center. There was no traffic and the road was unpaved and muddy. We came to some houses, and asked pedestrians we met about a hotel. They gestured on toward the lights. We may have walked a mile, our feet cold and wet, our packs feeling heavier with every step, before we came to the commercial district and found the *Residencial Varas,* a seedy little place that, by then, looked like The Ritz to us. Later, warm in dry socks and eating dinner with the Belgians, we talked about how much we appreciated our backpacks.

Packing for Hostelling or Car Camping

Packing for hostelling, if you won't have a car, is more of a challenge, since you must add bedding and a towel to the pile that has to fit in your backpack. Hostelling with a car is considerably easier. In that case, you may want to add a cooler to your luggage collection so that you can buy perishables for picnic lunches, and have a spot to chill white wine. In addition, carry a few kitchen utensils, plastic bowls and plates, camping flatware and—as a friend of mine recommends—buy a nice pair of wine glasses as mementos.

Camping is another story altogether. You'll need bedding and mattresses, a tent, a stove, and all the other assorted supplies for living like a nomad. In Hawaii we noticed German travelers arriving at the Volcanoes National Park campground one night with a metal kitchen box. In it they carried their stove, fuel, pots and pans, dishes, cups, utensils and staple food supplies. It was one of their pieces of luggage.

Nowadays, our luggage for extended camping in distant developed countries, consists of two large duffels, one cooler, and one kitchen box. We look like we are going on an expedition—and we are. The duffels have wheels so we can actually, between us, carry everything all at once from the baggage carousels to the curb. After that, we need a car.

Combination Trips

The only way to do both kinds of traveling in one trip is to find a place to stash the bulk of your gear you don't want or cannot carry. Bring backpacks with you to use on the portion of the trip when you will be using public transport, are actually backpacking in the wilderness, or just want to travel light for a while. Hostels and backpacker hotels are accustomed to storing luggage for people. For only a small fee, we have left duffel bags of gear for weeks.

Chapter Four
CHOOSING WHERE TO STAY

Finding inexpensive places to sleep at night is one of the most important tasks for frugal travelers—and *the* most daunting challenge. In most countries, the biggest percentage of a daily travel allowance goes toward paying for a hotel room. If you can't keep this cost down, your whole budget is sunk.

First, accept the fact that you can and must accept accommodations that are "sub-standard." Americans, I think, have gradually come to believe they are entitled to a certain quality of motel or hotel room. Hotels that meet American standards exist in probably every city of any size in the world, but they cost American prices. If you are passionate to travel and your budget does not allow for $75, $100 or more a night for a place to sleep, you can still go to all these same places and find a room for much less, but it will not meet American standards.

I met an American business man on a airplane once who complained to me that he hated traveling in Europe because in the smaller hotels he could afford, there was no direct telephone line from which he could dial the United States, there was a poor selection of TV channels, and the showers provided pitifully poor water pressure.

We had just spent a year of frugal traveling in developing countries. A hot shower of any sort was a bonus beyond belief. We never had televisions or telephones in our rooms, never mind judging their quality. I couldn't think of how to respond to his petty complaints.

Acceptance of low-quality hotels as a place to stay requires a redefinition of needs. Frugal travelers off to see the world do not need a beautifully furnished room, a television, a telephone, a nice view, a sumptuous bathroom, or even a hot shower—though one is always welcome.

What *are* the necessities? You may have your own list, but in our case we need a quiet room with a bed, a bathroom of some sort (possibly down the hall), and safety and security. Most of the time, nothing else seems important enough to warrant paying the extra expense.

Such basic requirements will not be acceptable to travelers who view accommodations as a crucial part of their trip experience. They expect to stay in places as good or better than what they have at home, and to be offered less would disappoint them. To them, a place to sleep is not a means to an end—a way of being in a new and interesting place—but an end in itself and an important aspect of the journey. This is understandable. I love finding rooms that are inexpensive and yet offer beauty, charm and comfort. However, for FITs, such rooms are like an unexpected gift. You are grateful and delighted, but you know they don't come along every day.

A vacationer, as opposed to a traveler, may be a person whose need for a high-quality room makes sense. A vacation suggests going someplace to settle in and relax. The accommodations *are* an integral part of the experience; but travel, particularly frugal travel, is generally not undertaken for relaxation. Its goals are experience, education, even enlightenment. You can (and should) try to create some relaxing days, but they are within the broader context of a challenging trip—which is anything but a "vacation."

No Reservations

Another roadblock on the way to finding cheap sleep is the fear factor. Finding inexpensive rooms generally requires you to travel without room reservations. There are exceptions. With fax, e-mail and easy international calling, the ability to make reservations yourself, even to stay in low-cost places, has increased in recent years. However, unless you have first-hand information you trust, you can't be sure this room will suit you. Furthermore, many of the smallest, least expensive places do not take credit cards, do not have fax machines, and, even if they are listed in guide books, may not take reservations. Although there are definitely times when an advance reservation for a room is a good idea, such as a late night arrival in a big city, in general FITs wing it. That's a scary idea for many people.

"What do you do if you can't find a room?" they ask. This is just about a nonexistent problem, in our experience. Unless you are unlucky enough to enter a city hosting the Olympics, you are going to find a room. Your guidebook should alert you to any times of the year when a particular place is likely to be crowded. You may need a reservation, for example, to visit Patzcuaro, Mexico during Los Días de las Muertas. Generally, though, even in the most popular tourist destinations, demand has created a supply. You will find a room.

My friend who wanted to go to Greece *did* go. She found the hotel rooms on the island of Santorini to be filled the day she visited but the police met the ferry, took the passengers without rooms to the police station, and matched them up with volunteer villagers who escorted them home for the night. She had a pleasant and memorable stay with a local family.

Whenever I get nervous about the day slipping away without our having secured a place to stay, George always asks me, "What is the worst thing that could happen?" I suppose I imagine spending the night on a park bench; but in reality the worst thing that has ever happened is that we had to take a room we didn't much care for, and had to go to the trouble of finding a new room and moving the next day.

The Advantages

Traveling without reservations and seeking inexpensive accommodations pays off in numerous ways. Sometimes you happen onto amazing bargains. We traveled by ferry to the Greek island of Paros one October with no idea where we would stay. A small boy met the disembarking passengers.

"Room?" he asked us. "Room?"

"Well. . ." we said, hesitating.

"Four dollars," he said.

We looked at each other. It might be worth taking a chance. "Okay," we said, and he set off at a scamper beckoning us to follow. When we could catch up with him we tried asking a few questions. Was there hot water? How far, exactly? But he had evidently used up his English, and just grinned and scampered.

After ten minutes of uphill huffing we came to a pretty little two-story house set alone in a field with a view of the sea and the whitewashed town of Paros below. We were given the entire upper floor, had our own bathroom with hot water, and even a refrigerator. Needless to say, we stayed several days.

In other cases, the payoff might be different. You might gain a story you will enjoy telling for years. One such experience for me took place in Inquisivi, Bolivia.

We were on a search for a hidden ruin of the Inca empire. Another traveler had told us she heard these ruins could be visited from Inquisivi, so we had made our way there by bus and truck with a pair of friends. The daily truck from the highway was an open lorry that quickly filled with mountain people on their way home. We lumbered for miles along a rough, dirt road through brown grasslands of the high Andes. Alpaca and llama herds looked up to watch us pass. Craggy snow peaks were on every horizon.

It was after sundown when we reached our destination. We asked the truck driver about a place to stay. The town had no

44

electricity. It was absolutely dark.

He pointed across a rough plaza. We went over and knocked on a door centered along an earthen wall. A woman opened it, showing us by candlelight to a large room off an inner courtyard. The room captained six cots; each rented for 86 cents a night. We asked about a bathroom and she pointed out chamber pots under the beds, a drain and a water spigot in the courtyard.

Just as we were settling down the door opened and the woman showed a man and his son into the room to take the last two beds. We recognized them; they had been on the truck with us.

At five o'clock in the morning a loud crowing startled me awake. It sounded like there was a rooster in the room with us. The noise continued for several minutes. No one but me seemed to care, so I got up to investigate. Maybe it was in the courtyard and I could chase it away, I thought. I opened the door and there was the rooster, tethered by his foot to a post. He had crawled out of a cloth bag. He must belong, I concluded, to the man with whom we were sharing our room.

Not willing to try stuffing this bird back in his bag, I returned to my bed and put the pillow over my head as the crowing resumed. A few minutes later the man and the boy left and silence and sleep returned. About 6 a.m., I awoke again with an urgent need to use the chamber pot. I had never used one before, but it seemed fairly straightforward. I pulled up my nightshirt and was about half finished when the door opened. The man and the boy were back. I suppose I had a stricken look on my face. Undoubtedly, it was red with embarrassment. In any case, the poor guy quickly backed out the door and I got back into bed to hide under the covers.

Later, I told the story at breakfast. Despite my humiliation, it was too funny to keep to myself. We never did find the ruins, but I'll never forget Inquisivi.

How to Find a *Good*, Cheap Room

If your guidebook doesn't lead you right to the door of the place you'd like to stay, sometimes it will get you to a neighborhood where you can make your own selection. In many towns and cities, the backpacking hotels tend to cluster in certain areas. Panajachel, Guatemala, is full of them. Khao San Road in Bangkok is another. Kings Cross, Sydney has several. In other places, you can find inexpensive rooms simply by walking the streets and looking for signs. In Chile people put a sign with the word *hospedaje* in their windows, indicating they are willing to rent out a room to travelers.

Tourist offices are great resources for finding inexpensive rooms. They will often provide you with a list of people that will rent out rooms, or a list of budget hotels, or even a map locating them around the city. If you aren't sure where to start when you get to a new town, hunt up the nearest tourist information booth. One lucky fact for Americans—they are almost always staffed by a person who can speak English.

"How do you ask for a room if the person at the hotel *doesn't* speak English?" people wonder. I do get hung up about communicating, but George reminds me, as I practice my Spanish before entering a small hotel somewhere in South America, that it is perfectly obvious what we want. Any idiot can figure out that two people with luggage coming into a hotel are looking for a room. Relax already!

What's really tough is using the telephone in a language in which you are not fluent. With luck, you can find someone else to do this for you. Tourist office staffers will generally call to see if a room is available for you if they've given you some hotel suggestions. They will also tell you what bus to take to get there, or draw you a map if you are going to walk.

With experience, you will be able to judge if a potential room will meet your needs. George and I avoid rooms facing busy streets if possible. In many countries the car, bus and truck traffic starts early in the day and is enthusiastic in its use of horns. Quiet is high on our list of needs.

We've also developed a subjective sense of how we *feel* about a place. Is the owner or staff person friendly and open? Or do we get the sense we are not welcome? Maybe this is a brothel instead of a real hotel, or maybe it's the local Mafia hangout. If it doesn't seem like we belong there, we don't stay.

We always ask to see the room before we plunk down any money. We suspect they will show us one of the better rooms, rather than simply booking us into any dark and dingy corner they can muster.

"How can you be sure a room is clean?" is a question frequently on the minds of potential frugal travelers. They want to save money, but the thought of dirt makes them squeamish.

I admit my standards of clean have degenerated since George and I began our frugal adventuring. I still appreciate freshly painted walls, brightly scrubbed tile, and the faint odor of pine-scented cleaner in the bathroom, but now I concentrate on clean sheets and a clean floor. If the paint is dingy and peeling, the doors are smudged and need the attention of a rag dipped in Fantastic™, if the furniture is worn and the linoleum scuffed —none of that matters if there's clean bedding and the room has been swept. Fortunately, this has always been the case, even in some of the most basic places. Universally, most people in the world have generous and kind instincts and most people prefer tidy and clean to dirty and messy. Hotel rooms reflect this, even if the room is a communal loft up a ladder in a Nepali trekking lodge—one of the most primitive places we've ever stayed.

Once I did question the cleanliness of the sheets on the bed in a hotel we had checked into—a small place in Katmandu. I was embarrassed when the inn keeper explained to me that the sheets were freshly washed even though they looked quite brown. They were stained from being washed, by hand, in the river.

I had a horror, in the early years, over the possibility of encountering bed bugs. The idea was repulsive. It would be unendurable, I thought. Then, we did run into them once, in a room we rented in someone's house in Chile. That morning we woke with scattered red welts on our middles. They didn't even itch. The reality turned out to be less upsetting than the fear. I am happy to say, that was the only time we had such an experience.

How to Increase Your Comfort

In budget hotels, mattresses are often uneven, saggy and/or thin. Pillows are generally huge, lumpy and hard. Individual climate control is lacking. The walls may be thin. In Nepali trekking lodges, sometimes the walls only go three-quarters of the way up to the ceiling. The German snoring next door sounds like he is in bed with you.

You can protect yourself to some degree from these hardships. Despite the pain of giving up precious pack space, George and I each bring a mattress, sleeping bag and pillow on our frugal travels. We use Therm-a-Rest™ brand air mattresses designed for backpacking. They are lightweight (1.5 pounds). Spread out over a bad mattress, they add immeasurably to our comfort. Fiber-filled sleeping bags, also in the lightweight backpacking style, can be used for comforters, or in really cold places, you can zip in completely. Our pillows are airplane size. They are usually much better than the bulky, offensive objects on the beds.

We first carried this supplementary bedding in South America, somewhat by accident. We were planning to backpack in Peru, taking the four-day trek along the ancient Inca trail to Macchu Picchu, so we had to bring our backpacking gear. When we discovered how significantly this gear improved the comfort level of the sleeping arrangements in low-cost hotels, we decided we would always carry such gear.

Burnout

Even with gear to improve comfort levels, night after night in spartan rooms can get depressing. Budget for an occasional splurge, if possible, or alternately, try harder for charm. I remember reaching such a point in Bolivia. The country is full of cheap, cement slab hotels called *alojamientos*. They are wonderful for staying in on a budget, but they are as ugly and utilitarian as can be. They are usually two or three stories high and built around a central courtyard, often full of parked cars, leaked crankcase oil and carbon monoxide fumes. Open halls connect the rooms, which look out on this cheerless, treeless court. Late one afternoon we arrived in Sucre, Bolivia after a long dusty day on the bus. We were traveling with another frugal couple, and they had quickly signed up for a room in one of these *alojamientos*. George and I inspected a room first. It was their typical room—about 8' x 10', two small metal beds, cement floor, small window, light bulb (20 watts) hanging from a wire, a grungy toilet and shower one floor down, and not even a nail to hang up a jacket. I sat on the bed and tears began to run down my cheeks. I was suddenly overwhelmingly depressed by the ugliness. I felt I couldn't stand three nights—our planned stay—in such a dungeon-like place. George looked at me in surprise. Usually, I was more stoic, a trooper, a dedicated member of the frugal team.

"Couldn't we leave our packs at the office here and look around a little more?" I tried not to sound plaintive. "Maybe there's something nicer at the same price . . . or close to it."

George did not understand me at all. Once he'd put his pack down, he could care less that there was supposed to be a place not far away that had bougainvillea just outside the window and a nice view. However, willing to be a loving spouse, he reluctantly agreed and we began an hour-long trudge around Sucre. We looked at six unpromising places before we finally discovered the Hotel Londres. It was an old, once elegant place with a large inner court where the gardens had been let go, but at least it had some trees and no cars. The rooms were large with high ceilings, tall windows, and even old, painted wardrobes. The floors were tiled, and a hint of Spanish colonial charm was still palpable in the air. It was almost as cheap as the alojamiento—under $10. I took great pleasure in the find. After one day at the *alojamiento*, our friends moved in as well. Finding the Londres was worth the effort.

One Night at a Time

Even if we expect to be in a place for more than a night or two, we resist paying or even committing to more than the first night in a room. We regard this as a test. Many reasons to move may show up.

In Panajachel, Guatemala, we found a room we liked very

much. It was above a small shop, it was spacious, and it had a view of *Lago Atitlan,* the beautiful volcanic lake in central Guatemala. That night, however, we discovered our mistake. The shop by day sold candy and snacks, but at night it turned into a local entertainment center. They showed video cassettes of American movies from 8 p.m. to 1 a.m.—at loud volume to—a large and boisterous audience. We couldn't wait to get out of there the next day.

Sometimes, even though we've found a room we are satisfied with, we keep looking if we expect to be there for several days. Hunting rooms is time consuming, but the effort can be part of the trip experience. We discover nice parts of town we might otherwise have missed, sometimes happening upon restaurants that look good for a future meal. We even learn more about the place we're visiting.

One time in Puerto Angel, Mexico—a little coastal town south of Acapulco—we had an adequate room, but I was hungering, once again, for charm. One small hotel could be only be reached by a winding footpath through a shady garden of flowers and trees. We went up to inquire about a room and at the top discovered a patio restaurant with an ocean view. They didn't have room for us, but we began coming over for breakfast after they served perfect pancakes topped with tropical fruit and yogurt. I asked where they got the fruit, since the only grocery store in town didn't have any fresh produce.

"The truck from Puerto Escondido comes in to sell every Tuesday and Saturday at eight in the morning" the señora told us.

Now we had a source of fresh fruit for our beach picnics as well as a great place for breakfast.

Success

Taking a chance on finding a room can be difficult for those who like to feel in control, and prefer the security of knowing things are already arranged. But taking a chance, bravely learning to risk and trust, are important skills frugal travelers need to develop. Serendipity is one of the biggest bonuses of independent travel. FITs aren't locked into certain rooms on specific dates in particular places. They can try this, or change their minds, and try that. If an engaging opportunity appears, they can take advantage of it. They are confident everything will work out just fine. And if it doesn't, what does it matter? A better room, perhaps with bougainvillea outside the window, may be just around the corner.

Chapter Five
CHOOSING WHAT TO EAT

"Don't *tell* me what you think it is," George said, as he munched eagerly on something he had just bought from a street vendor in Shanghai.

"But," I said, "It looks like . . ."

"No," he said. "I'm hungry and it tastes good. Crunchy. Want a bite?"

We knew by this point, three weeks into our visit to China, that the Chinese enjoyed as delicacies many foods we would prefer to encounter only as animals at the zoo. We also knew, as frugal travelers seeking to dine inexpensively by eating local food, we had to be open-minded. Occasionally, however, I drew the line.

"No, thanks," I said. "It looks like a sparrow to me."

It was a little bird, plucked and deep-fried in a sidewalk wok. George ate his, bones and all, as did the rest of the open-air diners gathered around this particular vendor. They spit out the beaks. I suggested we move on to the man selling something on a skewer that was less anatomically recognizable.

Frugal travelers don't necessarily have to eat sparrows in China to practice the frugal travel methodology for keeping down the costs of eating. Eating, like sleeping, is one of those unavoidable and potentially costly requirements of life that must be met on the road. If the eater, like the sleeper, insists on American standards in food, looking for familiar menus in a country where the diet is quite different from our own, he will pay dearly, probably won't get very good meals, and will miss out on a lot of fun.

The trick is to consider your exploration of new foods as an integral part of the adventure. Picky eaters—those unfortunates whose mothers used to cater to their finicky ways—may have trouble with this concept. They could end up like a friend of ours who went trekking in Nepal and didn't care for *dhal baht,* their rice and lentil staple of life. He lost 30 pounds.

You can dine frugally with ease if you eat simple and local food, pick restaurants with care, and sometimes prepare your own meals.

Eat Locally

Remember the story about the man who said he would never go back to Paris because he was uncomfortable in a restaurant fumbling around in French trying to order a meal? He was certain the waiter was laughing at him. A physician, and thus a person of stature and influence at home, he was accustomed to respect and threrfore unable to accept his inadequacy in this situation.

Not to get overly analytical about it, but such feelings happen. I get insecure when I venture into restaurants where I know I'm going to speak terrible Spanish while ordering a meal. And if it's a place like China where I can hardly say a word, I'm extremely anxious. George, again, is calm about this. He reminds me it's the same as when we enter a hotel and it's clear you are looking for a room; it is obvious when you go into a restaurant you are there to get something to eat. Furthermore, the people working at the restaurant are as anxious to sell you a meal as you are to get fed. Therefore, things will more than likely work out.

This has usually proved to be true. When you do have a communication problem in a restaurant, the best method for dealing with it is to acknowledge the problem and ask for help. The whole psychology of the moment changes. Instead of being the affluent and arrogant foreigner pretending to know what you are doing when you don't, you become a human being in need of aid from a waiter or a cook, and they are generally pleased to oblige.

During one of our early attempts at getting a meal in China we sidled into a small place trying to look inconspicuous. People were deftly shoveling in food with their chopsticks from platters heaped with steaming and delectable looking meats and vegetables.

Our mouths watered, but we didn't know how to get some for ourselves. We didn't see menus, waiters or waitresses. Instead there was a ticket booth. People would go to the booth, pay for tickets, take the tickets to the kitchen, and exchange them for food. We approached the ticket window, feeling dumb and smiling hopefully. The ticket seller was brilliant. She came out from behind her window and led us around the restaurant, pointing at various dishes and then looking at us. We would nod yes or no. (We caught on quickly.) Back at the window, she handed us tickets and wrote down how much money we owed. We paid, and got our food. Yea!

The next time, at another place, we were more prepared. We went boldly up to the ticket booth and showed the ticket person the characters in our phrase book for meat and vegetables. Of course, we didn't know what we were getting, but (except for the sparrow), we hadn't bought anything yet that wasn't wonderful. One meal I remember particularly, was a tray of twenty-four small, steamed, pork-filled buns in Shanghai that cost 16 cents.

During a trip to Greece we had a great experience in a tiny *taverna* in Athens. The menu was in Greek, no one there spoke English, and our waiter was perplexed about how to help us order. He had a conference with other staff members, then he gestured us to leave our table and follow him. In the cramped kitchen, the cook lifted the lid off several pots of aromatic dishes. He told us their names, which we could barely pronounce, and we made our selections. Everyone was happy—especially George and me.

In many countries the language is not as difficult to fathom as Greek or Chinese. Frequently a dictionary or traveler's phrase book will serve you well at a restaurant. It may take a long time to figure out what to order, but it's fun to try to translate the menu. Ask the waiter to help with pronunciation.

Sometimes it's better not to have an exact translation anyway. In Chile we ordered and ate something called *congrio* several times before we discovered what it was. It looked and tasted like an excellent, meaty white fish, but during a stroll through a market we came face to face with a large *congrio* hanging from a hook. It was a long, fat eel with teeth and a nasty expression on its face.

Be Patient

In many countries, small restaurants do not prepare food in advance of an order. In our experience, it is not uncommon to wait an hour for a meal. FITs will be happier diners if they see such periods as opportunities rather than delays. One solution is to invite other travelers who may be in the restaurant to join you at your table. The time passes quickly as you compare notes about your experiences. You can often glean great tips about places to go.

You can also pass the time productively if you remember to bring something to do. We write postcards, read guidebooks, study maps, write in journals, write letters, or even read the latest paperback novel we've found. It's not that we don't enjoy talking to each other but, after days of constant togetherness, we sometimes run out of things to chat about—at least temporarily.

How to Find *Good*, Cheap Restaurants

In many of the world's cities, commercial operations are grouped by type. It seems odd to us, but all the hardware stores will be on one block, the pharmacies on another, fishmongers somewhere else. Sometimes, small restaurants will also share a particular area of a city. Your guidebook should help you find such a neighborhood, if it exists; or you can ask for recommendations from your hotel keeper, the tourist office, or any friendly stranger who's trying out his English on you.

Another help is to stop and look at posted menus as you explore a town or city. Make notes (I carry a pen and notebook with me at all times) on those that sound good so you can find them when you get hungry. If menus aren't posted but a place looks interesting, we go in and ask to see the menu before we sit down. If the meals are priced higher than what we want to spend, we just leave.

In many Latin American countries a traditional noon meal is called an *almuerzo*. This usually consists of several courses, starting with soup, then meat, vegetables, pasta or rice, bread, and ending with a modest dessert (we've been served a plain banana or an orange on a plate). These meals are typically an excellent value, and what is even better, the restaurant has prepared vast amounts, ready to serve—fast food, Latin American style. The daily specials are posted outside, often on a chalk board, and restaurants vie with each other to tempt you in for their best offerings.

In many other countries, look for the daily specials. Sometime the menus for all three meals are posted outside or in the window, appealing to workday patrons. Look for them. The more willing you are to take the *soup de jour,* the more economical will be your meal.

Always Ask the Price

This point could be made in an aside in almost every chapter. It should be something of a mantra for the frugal traveler, for when you fail to heed it, you are often sorry. Travelers are obvious targets, and a few unscrupulous people will try to take advantage of you wherever you are. You may hate to go around constantly on your guard, suspicious of everyone, but caution should accompany your openness to the world. The times when we have violated this rule and *not* been punished for it are few—the Greek *taverna* is one. However, other times we've kicked ourselves after being stuck with an exorbitant bill. In the instance of food, it's a matter of not letting your appetite overwhelm your good sense.

In Bangkok, on our first visit, we asked a taxi driver to recommend a good, cheap seafood restaurant. Assuming he would do as we asked, we naively entered the one he drove us to without even looking at several others in the same neighborhood. Later we realized he probably got a tip for bringing us. The prices were not listed on the English language menu. We ordered, ate a nice meal, and then were socked with a tab way out of line. Dumb.

Since then, if we aren't clear about the prices at a restaurant, we get out that notebook and a pen and ask the waiter to write down what the cost will be before we order. We put our experience to good use in Chongqing. We were visiting the tourist information office located near the most elegant hotel in the city, called the People's Hotel, oddly enough. Perhaps we were feeling especially cautious in this location where well-dressed foreign visitors were much in evidence.

In any case, when we were approached by a handsome, friendly young man who spoke English, we were wary. He asked us if we'd like to have the local specialty, Mongolian hot pot, for lunch. We had been wishing we could try this famous dish, but at the hotel, where we had priced it, it was too expensive. He said he'd take us to a small place owned by his cousin where it was much cheaper.

"How much?" we asked.

"Cheap," he said, but would not get more specific.

We agreed to at least check out the restaurant with him. When we got there, a short stroll away, he sat down at a table and motioned us to join him. This seemed odd and our suspicions grew. The proprietor came over and our friendly contact ordered the hot pot.

"Wait a minute," one of us said, hating to be ungracious, but smelling a rat. "We want to know how much."

Much discussion ensued in heated Chinese. Finally we got a hard figure, which translated into about $10 each—a totally outrageous price for a ramshackle nook of a street restaurant with three tables. Remember the 16 cent platter of steamed buns!

We got up to leave. "Sorry, there's been a misunderstanding," we explained. "This is too expensive for us."

More heated discussion resulted in several lower offers, all of which we refused until finally an agreement was struck. We would pay $3 each, and there would be no charge for the "cousin's" meal. We pulled out the notebook for written confirmation. We knew we were still subsidizing our contact's lunch at this inflated price, but we were willing to go this far to sample the reputedly marvelous hot pot.

Maybe they were taking their revenge; I could hardly eat any of it. A beautifully arranged tray of food came. In a pot of oil, bubbling at our table over a bed of charcoal, we were to cook such delicacies as pig stomach, intestines, brains, liver and other unrecognizable body parts, as well as assorted vegetables and small, whole, bony fish. I wasn't eager to sample the pig parts, but I thought at least I'd enjoy the vegetables. Wrong. The oil was flavored with such hot chile that everything cooked in it came out so fiery it instantly burned my lips, mouth, tongue and good nature. George managed to eat a little more than I, but we were unimpressed with at least this example of Mongolian hot pot.

At least, we said, as we headed for the nearest noodle shop for lunch, we were only slightly ripped off.

Options When You Can't Cope with Local Food

We met a Brit in India who shared his disgust with us over travelers who didn't eat locally. "You know, I have run into people who go all over India eating at one Chinese restaurant after another. They don't *like* Indian food. Incomprehensible, don't you agree?"

"Mmmm," we said, looking sheepishly at each other. We were just such travelers, ignoring our own frugal travel conviction that eating locally was the best choice. We had tried Indian food many times, but had either had bad luck or just didn't know what to order. We're New Mexicans and enjoy hot green and red chile dishes, but we could not tolerate the searing heat of much of the Indian cooking we'd sampled. We were grateful to discover that in most towns we could find one or more Chinese restaurants serving mild rice and noodle dishes—filling and cheap. We felt they saved us from possible starvation.

Since that experience we've realized Chinese restaurants can be found in almost every town of any size on earth. When we've had enough of the local fare, whatever it is, we look one up. There can be peculiar variations. I remember carrots and peas turning up in many of the dishes served at a Chinese place in Bolivia. I suppose bok choy and bean sprouts are hard to come by in La Paz.

59

We didn't mind. It was a nice change from potatoes.

Avoiding Restaurants

In developed countries, eating three meals a day at restaurants, even modest establishments serving locals, can put frugal travelers over budget. You can control costs by putting together at least two meals a day from grocery stores or markets.

We bring a nylon ditty bag with that we call the kitchen bag. In it, we carry light weight-plastic bowls and sturdy plastic utensils made for backpacking. We also pack a camp knife, plastic cups, film-canister salt and pepper shakers, a couple of bandanas for napkins, a stash of reclosable plastic bags, and a leak-proof drink bottle or two. Thus equipped, we can purchase fruit, cereal, milk, yogurt, pastries, or whatever else appeals to us for our breakfast. We peel or wash the fruit back in our room with safe water.

Lunches are even easier, particularly in countries where bread and cheese are common. Add fruit and a drink and you have a meal.

Remember the friend who buys a pair of wine glasses when she arrives in a new country? She and her husband elegantly enhance their picnic lunches with wine in stemware. It's a challenge to carry them around without breaking them, she admits, but she has a growing collection of wine glasses with histories.

FITs on extended trips in developing countries may be persuaded to add a small backpacking stove and a pot to their kitchen bag. When you face a long bus or train ride, it's nice to have food with you that you can be fairly sure won't make you sick. We learned that boiling potatoes and eggs in our room the night before provides us with an easy-to-eat, tasty and nourishing meal, which we supplement with crackers, *chappati*, tortillas, or whatever the local bread might be, and bottled drinks and fruit.

A side benefit to market or grocery store eating is that you learn a lot about the place you are visiting. In New Zealand, for example, we saw evidence of the child-centeredness of the culture at the supermarket. Along with normal sized grocery carts sits a row of miniature carts, each festooned with a flag on a tall pole. Mom or dad sets off with the big cart and the youngsters follow, pushing their own. We couldn't decide if the flags were to help parents to keep track of their offspring, or to warn other shoppers to watch out.

In much of the world, however, you won't find grocery carts of any size—and no grocery stores, either. Lacking refrigeration, people shop daily in large markets, going from vendor to vendor to collect eggs, produce, grains, meats, spices, detergent and a pair of socks. Such a routine no doubt gets tedious for the local population, but FITs can take advantage of regional specialties for a meal or two each day. In India we developed a taste for tree-ripened mangoes. We would buy a small sack, take them back to our hotel, peel and then eat them leaning over a sink. Nothing is messier or more delicious.

In Guatemala we began a ritual of buying a large, perfectly ripe avocado at the market, along with a lime, onion and tomato each afternoon. We would find a quiet spot on the patio of our hotel, make *guacamole,* and munch it down with a small bag of tortilla chips and a rum and coke. We didn't even mind doing without ice.

In Chile, in the autumn, the abundance of fresh fruit in the markets presents an unforgettable tableaux for the taster or photographer. We made one meal a day of an assortment of fruit. Also, many Chileans are descended from pastry-baking European ancestors. A breakfast of their fruit strudels with several cups of *cafe con leche* is worth going to Chile to experience.

Tiny, tangy bananas are available in many tropical world markets. You have to eat them dead ripe, complete with brown spots, but when you do, they taste like a cross between an apple, an orange, and a banana.

Raw Food

The commonly invoked admonition to travelers, "cook it, peel it or forget it," is sound advice, particularly in developing countries where sanitation and refrigeration are marginal or non-existent. We avoid raw seafood, since ocean pollution is common in coastal waters and contaminated shellfish are more the rule than the exception. We peel fresh fruits, and we skip salads in restaurants, as difficult as that can be after weeks of traveling.

We fudge on this rule, however, on certain occasions and with precautions. The tomato in our Guatemalan guacamole, for example, has been washed by us in safe water (more about water in the chapter on health). We ate grapes and plums in Chile after washing them ourselves. Once in Bolivia, starved for an American style meal, four of us bought ground beef, lettuce and tomatoes, washing the vegetables carefully in pure water. We borrowed the family kitchen of our generous hotel keeper to make a feast featuring hamburgers and a huge tossed salad.

Street Food

Many travelers are nervous about eating street food (snacks or meals prepared and served from open-air booths and carts). Convinced that cooks cannot prepare healthful food without an enclosed and presumably more sanitary kitchen, they patronize restaurants only.

We found that travelers are as likely to be served unsafe food in a restaurant as from a street vendor. We were amazed to discover how many small restaurants in developing countries do not have the luxury of a refrigerator. They buy, prepare and sell perishable food on a daily basis. The potential for bacterial growth in food is probably just as great in such restaurants as in street carts. In fact, the only time I've become severely ill with food poisoning was after eating at a clean but refrigerator-less restaurant in Guatemala.

Do be careful about buying fruit drinks from vendors or restaurants. Unless you have the language to tell the drink maker that you do not want any water added to your drink, chances are tap water will be used to dilute it, or ice cubes blended in to chill them.

FITs can help contain food costs by eating judiciously from

street vendors. Ask yourself, is the food protected from contamination by flies, street dust, or other particulates? Is it served as soon as it's prepared? If your answers are "yes," you are probably going to be just fine. We have eaten street food in every country we visited where it's available, and have not suffered.

Actually, eating street food is one of the most fun things about travel in developing countries. If you are ever in La Paz, don't miss the fish tacos. I get hungry just thinking about how good they are.

The Sure-Fire Frugal Travel Diet

Potential travelers may be pleased to learn that the easiest way in the world to shed a few unwanted pounds is to take a low-budget trip to a developing country. A few weeks of eating locally (no access to the refrigerator and no tempting junk food) plus walking a lot, and you come home a slimmer, sleeker person.

Despite increasing attention paid to nutrition and low-fat eating in the U.S., we are still a nation of roly-poly people. Thirty percent of us weigh more than we should for optimum health. In developing countries, this is not the case. The diets in these countries usually consist of a lot of carbohydrates and not much protein. In Asia we lived on rice and pasta. We sometimes laughed about the heap of food on our plates supposed to be fried rice or noodles with meat and vegetables. After searching carefully for the meat, we were rewarded by occasionally finding a fleck of water buffalo or chicken.

When our children met us at the airport after six months of this, they claimed we looked like refugees. George had lost 20 pounds; I was down 10. We didn't mind at all. We were fit, healthy and thin. Whoopee!

Food at Home

Frugal eating in developing countries not only reduces your weight. It gives you a new perspective on shopping for food at home. I used to feel annoyed about the vastness of my neighborhood supermarket.

"Why do we need 45 different kinds of breakfast cereals?" I would gripe. "They take up so much space."

The abundance of food and the choices Americans have are unique in the world. When you have visited places where there arefew and sometimes no choices, you have a new appreciation for the American system of meeting this basic need with such efficiency and reliability.

You realize as well there's not much to complain about when it comes to the cost of eating in this country. The percentage of income spent on food is much lower here than it is in many other countries where people have far less money to spend. Frugal travelers have an excellent opportunity to learn this first-hand.

The train to Tarabuco

Chapter Six
GETTING AROUND

When local transportation is convenient and cheap, FITs don't rent cars. This can be a difficult concept for Americans to embrace. We are accustomed to the convenience of having our own wheels; renting a car at our destination is what we *do*. The idea of becoming dependent on some other method of getting around is often unthinkable. However, insisting on American standard hotel rooms and American-style access to an automobile, launches the travel budget into the ozone.

The advantages of going car-free are many. The first, naturally, is cost. Rental cars the world over cost about the same. Count on $30 a day or more. Add in gasoline, which in most every country in the world is significant. Even with a weekly or monthly rate it unlikely you would be able to do better than if you traveled within a country or region by public transportation—if it exists. In the developing countries of the world, people do *not* have one, two, three, four or five cars in their driveways or spilling out onto the street (depending on how many teenagers or still-dependent young adults live there). Instead, they get around as best they can on local conveyances. In these countries, government-subsidized subways, buses, trains, trucks and ferries will take you where you want to go for the same low price they charge the local citizenry. This is an unbeatable deal, and you might as well take advantage of it.

When to Rent a Car

In developed countries, renting, buying or leasing a car could be a reasonable option. In such countries, the public transportation is more expensive, and may actually cost as much or more than driving your own car. Furthermore, if through your research, you learn that camping is feasible, having a car will definitely allow you to travel in these developed countries for less. Staying in hostels or B&Bs (Bed & Breakfasts) may or may not require you to have a car. Look at public transportation options and costs carefully before deciding.

Arranging for a car, if you've decided it makes sense, can either be done before you leave home or after you arrive. If you have time to spend on a search once you arrive, you may get the best price by locating an English-language newspaper or asking for help from the local tourist office to shop for a car to buy, rent or lease. In many developed countries there are businesses willing to arrange a buy-back plan. You buy a car, signing a contract that requires the seller to buy the car back from you at a certain price after a specified length of time—assuming you have not wrecked the car. Compare terms, and check with the tourist office to make sure this business is reputable. Insurance will be required. Take time to shop around for that as well.

If you are short on time, you can often arrange such deals before you go. Consult your guidebooks, get on the Internet, or call the country's United States-based travel information service.

Why Not Rent a Car?

When George and I traveled in developing countries for a year, we were almost never inside an automobile. Believe me, it felt strange to come home and get behind the wheel. (For several days, I found myself thinking I should walk to the grocery store.)

Besides saving a lot of money by not renting cars, we discovered another, equally important reason for putting up with the inconvenience of not having one. We learned by putting ourselves in league with the local people, at the mercy, as it were, of the public transportation system, we gained enormously in our understanding of the place we were visiting. We obtained glimpses of local life and culture we otherwise would have completely missed. We had the opportunity to be, to some extent, participants in the pageant of life of the place instead of simply gawking observers. We had the chance to feel what it was like to be a Bolivian, a Guatemalan, a Chinese. When we look back, we don't remember the discomfort, the inconvenience. We remember other sharp moments etched in our memories that became significant parts of the experience as a whole. We learned that in many ways, getting around *is* the trip.

Fear Gets in the Way

Insecurity stops many travelers from embracing the concept that getting around *is* the trip. They fear getting lost, or they feel intimidated because they can't ask about the destination in the local language, can't ask fluently, or maybe they just don't like asking for help at all.

If this hits home, ask yourself what is the worst that could happen. Certainly you could get off the bus at the wrong place and not have any idea where you are. (That happened to us once in Guatemala and so we got on the next bus heading back the way we came and rode until we recognized the area.) Chances are you will not end up in some dark, forbidding, drug-infested neighborhood where you'll be robbed, stabbed, and dumped in a river.

More likely, if you do get lost, you will have to pay for a taxi back to a place you know—not a tragedy. Or you might have to ask several people to help you figure out what bus to take to get where you were going—in embarrassing Spanish, terrible Russian, or worse, plain English. That won't kill you either. Millions of people the world over want to practice their English, and are happy to be of service. They will be impressed because you are even attempting to get around on you own. Be courteous and speak slowly. Some helpers may be more eager than they are fluent.

It's surprising how few people in less-developed countries have any idea how to read a map, but they are fascinated by them. If you get one out to ask advice, a crowd may gather to look over your shoulder, but they will have little help to offer. Instead, they will stare at the map, argue among themselves, scratch their heads, and study the map with rapt attention. However, it will not be meaningful to them, and they won't be able to help you get you where you are going. Better to name a place, then ask which bus, which street, or which direction to take.

Once you do master the local transportation puzzle, you have not only a feeling of accomplishment but a powerful sense of freedom. You *know* how to do this. You can go anywhere in this city and get back to your temporary home. What a rush.

Successful FITs try to develop an adventurer's attitude. Maybe, they think, they'll discover a part of the city they would never have seen otherwise. Maybe they'll learn something about the bus system in this town. Or maybe they will meet someone willing to help who will also give them tips about what to see and do in this place—or even take them home and feed them lunch.

The hotel desk clerk or restaurant worker rule-of-thumb applies here again. When you get on a bus, the bus driver understands that you want to go someplace, even if neither of you can speak the other's language. You can blurt out, *"Museo de Artes?"* with your best accent and wait for a response. If he nods, get on. Hover near by, reminding him from time to time that you are still there and in need. *"Museo?"* Very likely he will tell you when to disembark.

We once had a bus driver in Nepal forget to tell us when to get off on an intercity bus. Thinking it had been too long and we may have missed our stop, we reminded him of our presence. "Bandipur?" we asked. With the Nepali equivalent of hitting his forehead, he stopped the bus, waited with us along the road until another bus came along headed back to the town where we wanted to go, flagged it down, spoke to the driver, and helped us climb on the roof with the other overflow passengers. He then instructed the new driver about what we needed, no doubt telling him we were a pair of helplessly stupid foreigners, then urging him to help us to our destination. We tried to relax and go with the flow. The ride back in the cool fresh sunset air was a particularly delightful half an hour. When we got off we uttered our only Nepali word, *namaste* (thank you) to our rescue driver.

How to Cope with the Inconvenience

Using local transportation will not cost much in currency, but it will be expensive in terms of time and convenience. If you are able to accept the premise that getting around *is* a big part of the trip, you will be able to accept these costs, and remain calm and delighted.

Buses won't run on the days you need them. Trains will be late, slow, bumpy or even cold. (If you ever take the train from La Paz to Potosí, be sure to bring warm jackets, socks, and even a blanket or an alpaca lap robe.) Adopting a positive, noncritical attitude will help immensely to make your transportation experiences pleasant.

Local transportation is as varied as the countries of the world. In Argentina, spiffy modern buses we took came equipped with hostesses in spike heels and short skirts. After the evening movie, she came around with a nightcap. In India, they had movies on some of the buses—featuring screaming women being carried off on the shoulders of bearded men. In Bolivia, one crowded bus we were on forded several rivers. In China we traveled by train, hard-sleeper class, slept in three-tier bunks and drank lots of hot tea. Peruvian trains depend on vendors to feed passengers. We bought hot, chewy corn on the cob—more like field corn than sweet corn, but good and filling.

You'll do best with local transportation if you quickly get a handle on how to get around in a new place. Guide books, local tourist information offices, hotel desk clerks and other travelers with backpacks are excellent sources of information about transportation options. The first thing we do in a city of any size is find out if there is a published bus or metro map, and how to get one. We enjoy the challenge of figuring out how to get around in a new place. It gives us a great feeling of control and confidence. George is particularly good at deciphering the codes and interpreting graphics. I am better, however, at sensing the direction we should turn when we emerge from an underground railway. As a back-up, we carry a compass. It is invaluable when you have a map but can't get your bearings.

Do You Really Need a Taxi?

In most airports of the world, you can usually find a cheaper alternative to a taxi ride to town. Find out before you go what these alternatives might be; it can save you many dollars in the first hours of your trip.

In Puerto Rico, for example, we had read about good bus service from the airport to San Juan—mainly to provide transportation to airport workers. When we landed we went straight to the tourist information desk. We asked where to catch this bus, and if it would take us close to the hotel where we had a reservation.

"You want to take the *bus*?" asked the girl at the desk. Most visitors, apparently, did not.

She gave us the directions we needed. For 35 cents each we rode clear across the city to the end of the line in old San Juan. Then we walked five or six blocks in the direction the bus driver pointed until we came across our hotel on the Plaza de Armas. A taxi would have cost $20.

Some friends of ours recently spent a week at a resort south of Cancun, Mexico. The resort offered to meet them at the airport, drive them to the resort hotel and back again. The couple, who did this before, said they could get there on their own. The local bus running south from Cancun cost 80 cents as far as the resort. The hotel charged $80. A little experience, information, courage and determination can save big bucks.

Hitchhiking

In some countries you can even get a free ride. We landed in the small town of Nelson on the south island of New Zealand and missed the shuttle bus. We had read, however, that this country was friendly and safe, and hitchhiking was possible. We set out, walking along the road to town. When we heard a car come up behind us, I stuck out my thumb for the first time in my life. The car immediately stopped, and the couple asked us where we wanted to go. They delivered us to the door of a hostel they said was the nicest in town.

We did some other hitchhiking in New Zealand with great success. We did not rent or buy a car in this country because we learned from the United States based New Zealand travel office that another cheaper option would work for us. After we arrived and knew our schedule, we signed up for backpacker bus tours. These buses provide a variety of destinations and schedules for low-budget travelers, stopping at night to stay in hostels. On one trip we took, the passengers pooled their money and trooped into a grocery store to shop for food to cook at a hostel, where a group meal was the tradition. Most of the tourists were students from Europe and the U.S., but they accepted us graciously. They said they thought it was neat that such old people would travel with them on the backpacker bus. At the time, we had just turned 50.

As comfortable as we were hitchhiking in New Zealand, we would not employ the practice just anywhere. The circumstances of each traveler and each country would determine whether or not this is a safe and acceptable option. A woman alone may not want to chance it, though we met a Belgian woman in Chile who had been traveling by thumb all over South America. She had studied Spanish intensively and was fluent, and she said she told anyone offering her a ride that she had no interest in a sexual encounter, and if this was what they were looking for, she didn't want the ride. She said she never had a problem, and in fact the truck drivers were particularly nice to her. I was in awe of her courage. We found couples get a ride a lot more easily than a man traveling alone. However, hitchhiking is frowned upon or even illegal in some countries. Know before you go.

The Train to Tarabuco

Exploiting local transportation options will reap enormous dividends in cost savings and rich experience. Some of our favorite and most vivid trip memories hang on transportation adventures. We will never forget, for example, our journey on the train to Tarabuco, Bolivia.

We were in Sucre and decided to visit what our guidebook called ". . .one of the most colorful Indian markets in South America." Convinced this was a must-see, we went to the tourist office to ask about alternative transportation. There were no buses, and a taxi would cost $40, we heard. Someone at the tourist office told us a train was leaving at 6:30 in the morning to travel the 70 kilometers. The tickets cost only 86 cents—one *boliviano* at the time. Bingo!

We were thrilled to have discovered this bargain, and decided to wait and have breakfast on the train. That way we wouldn't have to get up quite so early.

The next morning, waiting at the station, I was imagining the smell and taste of fresh *cafe con leche*, and pictured us sitting at a little table watching llamas and their colorfully-dressed herders from the train window. Then the train pulled into the station. We gasped in shock. This did not resemble any train we had ever seen. It was a single car that looked like a squat, ancient and decrepit bus outfitted with a cow-catcher and set precariously on little train wheels.

The waiting crowd began to cram itself into this tiny convey-ance. Not able to come up with a better idea on the spur of the moment, we joined them. There were not enough seats for everyone. We were left standing in the aisle. Well, not standing, exactly. Anyone taller than five feet two inches had to hunch over because of the low roof.

72

We set off, the driver shifting gears and using a clutch just as though he were driving a bus. George was fascinated. I was miserable. Not only was I bent over with people packed against me, I was having trouble staying on my feet as the "train" (I now thought of it as a train in quotation marks) lurched along. And what about breakfast? My stomach complained noisily.

I wasn't sure how I was going to endure three hours of this. I couldn't even see out. My view, unless I did a deep kneebend and tipped my head sideways, was of the track-side gravel.

Then a savior came to my rescue. A woman occupying about one tenth of the bench seat that ran across the back of the "train" tugged at my jacket. She gestured toward some bundles on the floor between the knees of the man beside her, tucked in against the seat in front of him. She seemed to think I could sit there. I looked at the man, who gave me a grin revealing several missing teeth. I took that as an assent, and gratefully arranged myself on the sacks of grain. I was touched by their thoughtfulness and thanked them in Spanish.

After about two hours we stopped at a small village and a few people got off. I stood up to stretch and relieve the strain on my arms—I had to clutch the seat-back next to me to keep from pitching into the lap of the man whose sacks were my seat. Then I spied an empty seat and grabbed it. For the last hour I enjoyed the spectacular scenery of the rolling *altiplano*, the Andes forming a dramatic background in blue.

When we got to Tarabuco, I photographed the "train," then grumbled to George about what a terrible trip it had been.

"Ah, but you'll never forget it," he said with a smile and a kiss. And we headed into town for some breakfast.

On the Bus in Guatemala

A uniformed man with a gun waved our bus over to the side of the road. We had just left the crowded streets of Guatemala City on a forty-mile journey to the quaint town of Antigua. "Now what?" we thought, feeling fearful.

The rest of the passengers did not seem concerned. As the bus pulled to a stop, those standing in the aisle lowered themselves to a feigned sitting position. The officer climbed on board, looked around, shrugged, got off and waved us on our way. In a moment the squatters were standing again. Could this charade have been lip-service accommodation to a government safety regulation that passengers were not allowed to stand on a bus? If so, the inspector must have been blind, or bribed, though we saw no money change hands. Such are the mysteries of life on Guatemalan buses. We were to discover more.

We traveled all over Guatemala by bus. Several lines covered the country thoroughly, frequently, and at very little cost. One day we made our way to Guatemala City's main bus terminal, looking for a way to get to *Volcan Picaya*, a smoking volcano we were hoping to climb. Dozens of buses filled the area and the crowd was thick. If an organizing principle existed in the chaos, we could not discern it. In fumbling Spanish, we asked a young man if he knew of a bus to San Vicente de Picaya, the little town on the slope of the semi-active peak. He looked quickly around, then suddenly sprinted off after a bus that was just pulling out. The bus stopped, we rushed up, and the young man scrambled onto the roof to take the packs we handed up, grinning at his success. We gave him a few *quetzales* for a tip and felt grateful for his effort on our behalf.

Another day we were in Panajachel (on beautiful *Lago Atitlan*, set in a ring of still smoking volcanoes) planning a move to Quetzaltenango. The trip was complicated. We had to get off the bus at a certain crossroads and flag down another bus, our hotel keeper told us. The second bus would say Xela (shay-la). Guatemalans did not accept the government-selected name of Quetzaltenango, he told us. They preferred the ancient Indian name of Xela, which they use in defiance of the government.

On this, as on most of the buses we rode there, we were the only foreigners. Here, away from the city, the people dressed in colorful, village-specific clothes. Embroidered blouses, hand-loomed skirts, or fancy, decorated pants identified where they came from as surely as if they were wearing a sign. The women's *huipiles* (blouses) served as purses and tote bags. From them they pulled bus fare, food or even fresh diapers for their babies.

At a brief stop, a small, brown, rosy-cheeked boy with black button eyes climbed onto the bus, sang a lilting little song, then passed around his dirty and unraveling stocking cap. Something about that moment grabbed me. Maybe it was trying to comprehend the need that would move me to send either of my precious little girls to do something like that to supplement the family income. Tears stung my eyes as I dropped a coin in his hat and tried to get him to look into my eyes. He did not.

Down the curving road we sped toward Xela. As he headed into one turn, the driver sounded his horn several times. Nothing was in the way. Instead, he was summoning a scrawny dog who came racing up to the highway. The driver slid open his window and tossed out a tortilla. The dog grabbed it in flight. The driver laughed out loud. He and the dog, it seemed, were old friends. Why did I want to cry again?

A couple of days later we were jouncing along on a bus to Huehuetenango, amused when we noticed our driver had blocks on the pedals so he could reach them. The relatively small native people had a hard time fitting into the recycled North American buses they were driving—many of them old school buses. We passed through the village of Salcaja and saw weavers outside working with thread strung on posts that reached 100 feet up a hillside. We looked at each other and leaped to our feet, asking the driver to stop. We got off knowing, after all our Guatemalan bus experience, that we could easily flag down another bus later.

We spent half an hour with the weavers. They not only showed us how they set up these primitive hillside looms to design the *muñecas*—the prized human figures that appear in the best-quality Guatemalan fabric—they took us into their houses, offered us coffee, and showed us how the tied and dyed black and white thread was woven into the final cloth on floor looms in dimly lit, tiny workrooms. This fabric, they told us, would bring them about $40 for a five-yard piece.

Our fifteen-year-old daughter joined us for a few days during her winter break from high school. On Christmas day the three of us rode from Antigua to Guatemala City and then on to Livingston on the Atlantic coast. The buses this day were even more crowded than usual, as families journeyed here and there for the holiday. Three and even four people squashed themselves into seats meant for two. The air was stifling. A man standing in the aisle who had too much to drink scrambled over several people to throw up out an open window. The driver stopped and, with some difficulty, evicted the man, who stood by the side of the road with a bewildered smile as we drove away.

I looked at my daughter, squeezed up against the window. She was in tears.

"What's wrong?" I asked, expecting her to tell me she was uncomfortable, grossed out, and sorry she ever came.

She said. "I had no idea places like this even existed. I'm so glad I came. I feel so different. How will I ever explain it to my friends? Our problems seem so trivial now."

Near the end of our stay in Guatemala we ate a meal at a nice restaurant in Flores, the town closest to the Mayan ruins at Tikal. A freshly-pressed American couple and their guide sat near us. They appeared to be about our age—late forties. A taxi waited for them outside. It was clear they were not on a low-budget trip.

They were fretting about how long the food was taking. George and I looked up from our books to talk with them. They told us they flew in for a visit to Tikal on a small plane from Antigua where they had been staying in a charming old hotel. After their meal they were to fly to Guatemala City for their flight home.

Later George and I said we could hardly comprehend how different their trip was from ours. They had come and experienced a week of pampered ease. No struggles, no discomfort. They had not been on even one Guatemalan bus. Their trip, we said, must have been enjoyable. Very pleasant, even luxurious. But much to our surprise, we realized we did not feel envious, but rather a little sorry for them. Our month on the bus was rich in experiences we would have been loathe to give up. We would not have traded places with them even if we had the chance.

Over the Zoji-la in a Tata

Getting around was so much of the trip in Guatemala. The same thing was true during our weeks in India. We had one experience vividly illustrating the point that rewards come to FITs who take the risks associated with no-reservation, free-wheeling, take-it-as-it-comes public transportation. Even when situations seem truly desperate, solutions can emerge that work out much better than anything you could have imagined or planned.

We were lucky enough to be in India during a period when travel in the northern state of Kashmir was safe for travel. Since then, armed rebellion has made it dangerous. We wanted to travel between the town of Srinagar (in Kashmir) and Leh, in the neighboring state of Ladakh. To get there, we had to cross a section of the Himalaya with several passes, a major one of which was called the Zoji-la. A narrow stretch of dirt and gravel crosses its 16,000-foot height. The road was traveled mostly by trucks—colorfully decorated, boxy little affairs with small engines made by a company called Tata. The trucks, a couple of buses a day and a few cars made their way over this 200 miles of often perilous road for only six months each year. In winter, the snowy pass was closed and the only link between Srinagar and Leh was by air.

We got on the daily bus on a summer day in 1988 for the 24-hour trip—spending one night on route. We spent several weeks in Leh, trekking, visiting Buddhist gompas, and becoming acquainted with this intriguing outpost of Tibetan culture.

When it was time to head back to Srinagar and then Delhi for the next leg of our journey, we discovered a problem. The pass had been closed for several days by a landslide. On top of that, flights had been canceled because of high winds. No one could leave. Now the pass was open, but a backlog of travelers wanted to get out. Frantic foreigners, trying to make international flights out of Delhi, swarmed around the bus station hoping for seats when there were none to be had. Daily flights had resumed, but the waiting list had dozens of names. We were stuck in Leh.

Talk buzzed among visitors in the restaurants and small hotels. We learned we could share a taxi with two or three other people, but the taxi drivers were asking $300 to make the trip. Then we heard if you visited the lot where the trucks parked overnight before starting their trips back to Srinagar, you could sometimes buy a ride from one of the drivers.

George and I and a German trekking friend named Barbara walked to the lot after dinner. Several drivers gathered around soliciting our business. We settled on a friendly Sikh in a red turban who spoke a few words of English. His truck had "Lucky Tent House" written on the side. He asked 80 rupees each (about $6.) We were to be back at 5 a.m.

In the morning we discovered our driver, Jogmohinder Singh, had also sold rides to a French couple. None of us were overjoyed as we squeezed into the narrow seat behind the driver and his assistant. It would more comfortably have accommodated three. At least the couple was getting out at Lamayuru, a gompa a mere six hours down the road.

Singh started his Tata, lit an incense stick, set it on the dash, said a prayer, adjusted his turban, and we were off. As we rumbled out of town, he removed his dress turban for a working green and white checked one that he deftly wound while driving. Squashed behind him, we five smiled happily. This was definitely a high ranking travel experience.

After the French couple got off, we stopped for lunch. Alongside the road, Singh and his assistant cooked a vast pot of potatoes, rice and greens. George, Barbara and I dug into our rations. We had brought boiled eggs, tuna, crackers, apples, pears and cookies.

It was harvest season in these high valleys. As we journeyed we saw human haystacks moving slowing along the road. Oxen yoked together, walked in a circle to thresh the grain with their hooves. It was like a medieval tableaux.

As darkness gathered the assistant lit two joss sticks of incense, waved them over the four decals on the windshield (a figure riding a lion, another on a horse, and two veiled, ethereal female dancers), then passed them over the dash, the brakes and the clutch, set them in their hole in the dash and clasped his hands together. It was a relief to know everything would continue to work properly.

Then, when we reached the graveled, one-way stretch of the road over Zoji-la, we learned we would have another 24-hour delay—there had been another slide. The army was clearing the way. We set up our tent near the truck. In the morning we woke to find hundreds of trucks packed around us. The back of the empty Tata became our headquarters. The curious came by all day to see what we were doing. Some peered over my shoulder to watch me write in my journal.

Our camp stove attracted much attention. We had several offers to buy it, as well as our shoes. We were happy we had brought extra food. Dried soup, potatoes, carrots, kohlrabi and onions were in our food bag.

Singh brought an English-speaking driver over to translate for him so he could tell us he wanted more than anything to be a truck driver in the United States. Could we use our influence as American citizens to get him a visa? He had applied many times, he said, and had been turned down.

Jogmohinder Singh, like many of his countrymen, worked at a grueling job for low pay. He earned $50 a month traveling these dangerous roads. He could see no way to improve life for himself and his family. His assistant received $10 a month plus free room (he slept in the truck) and board (Singh's cooking). We tried to picture them thundering down an interstate at home in an 18-wheeler. The Tata was like a VW bug in comparison. It was painful to become aware of the hopelessness they felt and it was a burden almost greater to bear than the poverty that fueled it. I knew we couldn't get him a visa, but I wished I could at least have promised to send back opportunity and hope.

We made our beds that night on the roof of the truck's cab in an open cubbyhole. Around 11 p.m. hundreds of truck engines sputtered to life and the drivers began jockeying for position. We

79

all had to pass through one gate, making it a pointless struggle, but no one was willing to hang back and wait. With the assistants calling out instructions, the trucks inched forward, almost touching. They blocked each other whenever they could, yet there was no malice or verbal abuse. It was like a bizarre game. Dust swirled, exhaust fumes rose and din assaulted our ears as we watched the drama in amazement. More than an hour passed before a soldier waved us through the gate and we joined the line of trucks snaking up the switchbacks above us in a midnight Himalayan parade.

We snuggled into our sleeping bags on our mattress pads and slept.

Chapter Seven
TAKING CARE OF YOUR HEALTH

Frugal travelers stay healthy by taking precautions appropriate to their destinations. Long trips to less-developed places, may require elaborate preparation. For short trips, or journeys to more developed countries, preparations can be kept fairly simple.

Research

The first step in determining the level of precautions required on a particular trip is to learn about the local health hazards. The latest and best word on the subject is published by the Centers for Disease Control and Prevention (CDC), of the Public Health Service of the U. S. Department of Health and Human Services on their web site at www.cdc.gov. You can also order an annual book *Health Information for International Travel,* to look up your destination for a general assessment. Then you can request their biweekly *Summary of Health Information for International Travel.* Call 404-639-3534 or 800-311-3435 or see their web site at www.cdc.gov.

If you are going to western Europe or similarly developed countries, they will tell you not to worry. Travelers can rely on their information about what immunizations or boosters they need, the safety of the tap water, and other considerations regarding health.

FITs who are off to less developed areas, however, will want to buy the CDC book and study it carefully (or print out material from the web site) for helpful information.

No matter what your destination, there are several things you need to do and know.

Join IAMAT

The International Association for Medical Assistance to Travelers (see Appendix for address) provides, for a donation, both membership and an invaluable booklet. The booklet contains an annually-updated list of English-speaking (and often U.S., Canada or U.K. trained) physicians located by city and country. If you should become injured or ill, this brochure will help you find a doctor with whom you can communicate.

Through IAMAT the traveler can also purchase detailed information about the climate and public health issues of their destination country or region.

Treating Travelers' Diarrhea

Digestive upheaval is the most common health problem of travelers. It can occur no matter how sanitary or developed the destination country. In fact, George and I both experienced diarrhea on returning to the United States after being in Asia for six months. The human digestive tract is sensitive, and any sudden change of water or food can trigger temporary distress. What we have learned, and what the CDC recommends, is that often the best treatment is no treatment at all.

When we set off on our year-long trip, I was adamant about travelers' diarrhea. I wasn't going to put up with it. I obtained a preventative prescription of Bactrim™, an antibiotic used to treat digestive bacteria causing diarrhea. At the first sign of distress, I planned to zap the offending bugs with my drug. Take that, I would gloat, proud of my weapon.

The trouble was, my plan didn't work. I got sick, felt lousy, took Bactrim™, felt better, then get sick again.

Meanwhile, George was experimenting by taking no drugs at all. He would treat his digestive upsets by temporarily fasting and drinking water and tea. Soon he was *staying* well.

Eventually, we decided it's best not to treat travelers' diarrhea with drugs, but to accept it as a common consequence of traveling. Deal with it by eating and drinking things that help your body to cope. Gradually you will develop the tolerance you need for the local digestive flora and fauna, and you will have fewer and fewer problems.

When my children were small their pediatrician recommended what he called the "BRATS" diet to soothe an upset digestive tract. It works like a charm for travelers too. Bananas, Rice, Apples, Tea and Skim milk was his BRATS diet. Bananas, rice and tea are particularly easy to obtain in most countries. (Canned applesauce is often available.)

If you are carrying a camp stove, you can even fix rice in your room if you feel too terrible to go out to eat. George has done this for me more than once.

Pepto Bismol™ tablets also work well to relieve symptoms and do not compromise the ability of the digestive tract to adapt. We also carry the prescription drug Lomotil™ (or substitute Immodium AD™ or a generic) to control symptoms if we are faced with a day-long trip.

Persistent diarrhea with fever may call for a more aggressive approach. Seek medical help. However, if no medical help is available, try Bactrim™ or other digestive tract antibiotics.

Persistent diarrhea may also be caused by a parasite, *Giardia lamblia*. If so, neither eating gently nor an antibiotic will cure you—the treatment required is an antiprotazoan. Generally, this illness does not develop until some days after exposure. If you are at home, you can be tested. If not, it is sometimes recognizable by mucous in the stool and a sulfurous odor. On a long trip to a place with few treatment options, you may decide to carry an antiprotozoan for emergency treatment, but a definitive diagnosis is not possible without a lab test.

We had corroboration of our travelers' diarrhea theory during our visit to Nepal. When we arrived in Katmandu we had been in Asia almost five months. We had experienced occasional bouts of digestive upset, but by then we seemed to have developed bowels of iron. While travelers who had come directly to Nepal from Europe or North America were dropping like flies along the trail, we ate everything put in front of us (though we were careful about water) and kept on trekking.

All this talk about digestion may seem excessive, but problems of this sort are so common and so disruptive to a happy experience, it is worth doing everything you can to minimize your risk. Count on it. Visit a developing country for more than a few days and you will get *tourista*. Realize it's probably not going to keep you down for long, and take the action described here. Chances are you will soon be acclimated and sturdy of bowel.

Staying Healthy in Asia, Africa and Latin America, a book by Dirk Schroeder, contains an excellent and more lengthy discussion of this and other travel-related health issues. See Appendix.

Vitamins and Remedies

My personal inclination is to pack vitamins and take them everyday. I take a high-powered multi-vitamin with minerals, supplemented with extra C and calcium if I don't expect to eat many dairy products. Travelers are often taking precautions against eating raw fruits and vegetables, so they may not be eating as many as they do at home. Thus a supplement, even if you do not bother at home, makes sense.

Carry prescription or herbal remedies according to your personal needs and the destination. Trips to underdeveloped countries call for a more extensive pharmacy. Legally, you are required to carry prescription drugs in their original containers. This can create a lot of bulk. Ask your pharmacist to package your pills in the smallest possible bottles, wrapping the labels around them, even overlapping if necessary. However, be sure the essential information is readable.

Many guidebooks also advise you to carry a letter from your physician listing all prescribed drugs and why you have them. We have never been asked to produce such a document, but if you have a large stash that may arouse suspicion at customs, it wouldn't hurt to have it.

A Personal Pharmacy

Yours will be specific to your own needs and wishes, but here is what we carry, and this list is similar to what Dr. Schroeder recommends in his book. First is a list of prescription drugs.

1. A broad-spectrum antibiotic. We take Keftabs™ on long trips to remote destinations. We have not had to use this ourselves, but we did treat a fellow trekker who had a nasty infection in his leg.

2. A muscle relaxant. We like Norflex™. In our experience, frugal travelers hoisting backpacks onto bus rooftops or hauling them up and down narrow staircases may pull, strain or otherwise injure a muscle. This drug helps promote a rapid cure.

3. Sleeping pills. A "velvet hammer" sleeping pill—as our physician describes strong, prescription-type drugs—are helpful to have in emergencies. On an all night plane, bus or train trip where sleep is elusive, we pop a pill to feel more human the next day. To adapt to an eight- or ten-hour time change, we use these sleep aids at bedtime for a couple of nights. After that, we depend on a one milligram tablet of melatonin, the natural sleep hormone, for another few nights, or until we feel jet lag is resolved.

4. Pain medication. Again, for emergencies, it's nice to have something strong as well as the usual over-the-counter headache medicines in your first aid kit. I carry Tylenol™ with codeine.

5. Seasickness medication if you have such tendencies and expect to undertake any voyages.

6. For underdeveloped countries, try to get an eye antibiotic ointment.

A First-Aid Kit

Where you are going and what you expect to do there will determine how extensive a first-aid kit you should prepare. Tropical destinations require sunscreen, lip protection, insect repellent, insect bite treatment, and an anti-fungal for athlete's foot. For the beach we also bring a vial of vinegar. Nothing works better to prevent the common infections resulting from coral scrapes than a thorough washing with soap, clean water, and vinegar rinse, and a topical antibiotic ointment (should be in any first aid kit.) Here's a good checklist:

► FITs, likely to walk a lot, should pack a good supply of Moleskin™, a Dr. Scholl's product that prevents blisters if you apply it to a hot spot before a blister actually forms. If you are too late, cover if with a non-stick Telfa™ pad, then Moleskin™.

▸ Take plenty of Peptol-Bismol™ and a stronger anti-diarrhea medication such as Lomotil™ or Immodium™.

▸ Include a thermometer to monitor a fever.

▸ Take an assortment of bandages.

▸ You need a sterile wash for wounds.

▸ Triple antibiotic ointment.

▸ An eye wash and cotton swabs in case of soot in the eye.

▸ Tweezers, a needle, and a magnifying glass for penetrating thorns or slivers.

▸ Over-the-counter therapies for colds (Sudafed™ or Actifed™ are two).

▸ Allergy medication.

▸ Fever remedies (aspirin or Tylenol™).

▸ Pain medication for aches or swelling from injury (ibuprofen).

▸ Skin rash ointment containing hydrocortisone.

▸ Those with allergic reactions to insect stings may want to carry adrenaline and a disposable injector. A mild reaction can often be treated with Benedryl™ tablets to prevent hives or swelling.

▸ In some countries disposable needles for injections are not used. In such places, the risk for disease transmitted by needles is significant. If you are going to such countries, you should carry your own disposable needles, with a letter from your physician. Insist they be used if, in an emergency, you need any injections.

▸ In these same countries the purity of the blood supply may be uncertain. Avoid a blood transfusion if at all possible. Sometimes plasma expanders can be substituted for blood temporarily, says the CDC, until you can get home or to a place with safe blood. These issues are discussed in the CDC guide.

Malaria

Tropical destinations often require malaria-prevention drugs. New strains of the disease are resistant to older malarial prevention drugs. If you are going to a malaria area, be sure to discuss preventative drugs with an infectious disease specialist who has the most up-to-date information. These drugs must be started before you leave home and continued for some time after you return.

The second front in the defense against malaria is preventing the critters from biting you in the first place. They are mainly nocturnal, so if you are out in the evening, be sure to wear long pants and long-sleeved shirts, and rub exposed flesh with repellent such as Johnson's Off™.

One problem encountered by frugal travelers is that windows on small, family-owned hotels and guest houses in many tropical places are not screened. We believe it is essential to carry mosquito netting to drape over beds. We have slept in many rooms in places like Thailand, India, southern China, Guatemala, Costa Rica, southern Mexico, and the lowlands of Nepal, where no screens were on the windows, no netting was provided, and malaria-carrying mosquitoes were common.

From a camping supply catalog (Campmor) we bought a double-bed sized netting supported by two fiberglass tent poles and tucked into the mattress. Often we had to push two twin beds together to use it. This was an invaluable addition to our gear, even if it was only to keep from having mosquitoes of any sort whine in our ears—not to mention drink our blood.

On a recent trip to Southeast Asia, we discovered we didn't need our netting if the room was equipped with a good fan. Leaving the fan on all night kept the "mozzies" from being able to land on us. However, it's a bit annoying to sleep under a sometimes noisy fan, and I don't care for the constant wind. I prefer netting—unless it is so hot you need the fan anyway.

Another parasite found in tropical developing countries that is worth making an effort to avoid is the one causing Schistosomiasis. This villain goes from a snail host in fresh water to a human host—where it causes great harm. Do not swim or bathe in fresh water lakes, streams or ponds in tropical environments. Too bad if you have to stay out of that inviting pool under a waterfall, but I wouldn't take a chance if I were you.

Even in developed places hazards lurk in fresh water pools. You will be adequately warned if you are hiking there. In Hawaii, a disease called Leptospirosis can enter your body through any open wound from fresh water pools and streams. This vermin has killed several healthy Hawaiians.

Health Insurance

Not all health insurance will cover you if you become ill or injured in another country—Medicare for one. If your insurance does not cover you, policies are available with widely varying coverage. The problem for frugal travelers, however, is that most of them are costly. Doing the cost/benefit analysis is not easy.

First, assess your own health care needs. If you are in good health and are unlikely to need medical evacuation or emergency hospitalization, you may be willing to take a chance and skip it.

Most serious medical emergencies for travelers involve accidents. Consider buying an emergency evacuation policy only. Such policies will evacuate you to the nearest hospital with Western medical standards, or home ("medical repatriation") depending on what is medically necessary. You and your insurer may not agree on the action needed, so be sure to address the issues when you purchase the insurance. See the Appendix for the names of some companies that sell travelers' insurance. Costs run from $21 for a policy good for a trip of from one to eight days, to $162 for a policy in effect for a year, but valid for trips up to 90 days in length. It's harder to find coverage for longer trips. It does exist, but it costs more.

Health insurance is often sold separately from evacuation insurance, though it can be included. Expect to pay from $500 for a year of coverage on 90 day trips, to $466 a month for full coverage. Many options are available, and costs may depend on your age and destination. Call the companies listed and ask for their brochures, then call them back when you understand the various options.

Do check out the health care available in the country or region you are visiting. Enlightened places with national health care may extend their low-cost or free care to visiting foreigners as well as their own citizens. Country-specific guidebooks will answer your questions.

Accidents

Motorcycle accidents, not malaria or some other disease, are the leading cause of death among Peace Corps volunteers, according to Dr. Schroeder. Accidents in general are the most significant cause of health care crises for travelers.

Some accidents are not preventable, but it is wise to travel with a heightened awareness and caution. If you do rent motor-scooters or motorcycles, make sure you wear a good quality helmet, says the doctor. Assess every situation for potential danger, and have a response plan in mind. In rickety old hotels, keep a flashlight handy and know how you will get out in case of fire. In boats with no life preservers, an air mattress will support you. If you have one, keep it nearby. Be aware that in many countries, pedestrians do *not* have the right of way and you are in danger when you cross a busy highway or street.

We had several near calamities during our year of frugal travel which may serve to illustrate the unexpected dangers you can face. Mostly, it was good luck that saved us rather than any vigilance on our part.

On the hilly streets of La Paz, cars with drivers are not the only hazard. One evening we turned a corner to see an empty vehicle rolling down the steep street toward us. It was traveling backwards with its passenger door open and sweeping the narrow sidewalk. We were paralyzed for a second or two, then turned and ran. George tripped and fell. I screamed at him to get up—a big help. Just in time we dodged into a doorway to escape. Damage: one skinned knee.

We had a run-in with a bicycle in Oaxaca, Mexico. We had

arrived on a bus and were walking side by side on a narrow sidewalk looking for a hotel. George was on the street side, facing traffic. Some cyclists came toward us. All of a sudden, George was sprawled on the ground, lying on top of his backpack. Next to him lay a student and his bicycle. They picked themselves up and discovered the bike hand brake had caught on a dangling loop of strap from George's pack. The resulting jerk threw them both in a heap. The bicyclist was annoyed with George, which we thought was rather unjust. Happily the victims suffered only a few scrapes and bruises.

A horse-drawn carriage gave us a scare in Viña del Mar, Chile, only a day after we began our year-long trip. Again, George took the brunt of things. (I'm not sure why he seems to be the more accident prone.) It was late in the afternoon when we set off on a town tour. The horse was cantankerous, wanting to head for his stable and some hay, no doubt. He refused to cross a bridge —it was leading away from home. At the time, we didn't realize this was the problem. I thought he was balking because what he was pulling was too heavy. As the driver hopped down to try to lead him across the bridge, two of us got off too, to lighten the load. The horse reared up, shook off the restraining hand of the driver, and ran away. George and another passenger clung to the flimsy buggy and tried to secure loose daypacks and cameras.

George claims he acted without thinking, but I am sure he must have been inspired by Saturday afternoon matinees from his childhood. He climbed over the driver's seat of the rocking carriage and onto one of the wooden shafts next to the horse. He reached down for the trailing reins, climbed onto the horse's back, grasped the other rein, and pulled him to a stop. He tied him to a lamppost for the pursuing driver, and calmly gathered our things and walked back, the other passenger with him. It seemed like a miraculous survival to me.

My only mishap was a severely sprained ankle in Nepal. A few days rest at a picturesque village, with treatment by a visiting French doctor, and I was able to walk out.

Water

Do *not* drink tap water in developing countries. It may be safe, but it may not. Waterborne diseases, like cholera, can be serious or even life-threatening. Bottled water is becoming widely available even in developing countries, so chances are you will be able to buy safe drinking water. However, if you expect to be in remote areas with few or no towns, you may need a backup water treatment plan. Bring along any necessary equipment and chemicals.

One possibility is a water filter. We carried a Swiss Katadyne™ to Asia and filtered mountain stream water or well water when boiled water wasn't available. The CDC does not recommend water filters. Some are just not good enough to do a thorough job; and even the best, unless they have a chemical iodine attachment, may allow passage of the hepatitis A virus as well as diarrhea-causing viruses. Safer options are available.

One of them is to treat your drinking water with iodine crystals. Outdoor stores sell iodine solution water treatment kits. They are effective and convenient. Be sure to let the water sit for a sufficient amount of time, as explained in the kit. Too much iodine, however, is poisonous. It is fine for occasional use, but for an extended trip, you should not use this method of purification. Besides, it makes the water taste bad.

The best method is to boil water. On an extended trip, it's a good idea to have a camp stove anyway. Be sure to get one that will burn kerosene or unleaded gasoline rather than only refined white gas camping fuel—readily available at home, but not in many developing countries. Boil the water for five minutes (longer at higher altitudes), and keep it in a container you have cleaned with boiled water.

If none of the above appeals to you, you can always try to get along drinking bottled beer, canned soft drinks, hot tea and coffee. We've been known to brush our teeth in tea when we were really desperate.

Cleanliness

You can do a lot to stay healthy by being extra careful about washing your hands before eating. Carry a bar of soap in your daypack, and use it. No towel? Bring a bandana. I've also learned that my hair works well as an emergency hand dryer!

Even better, carry a small bottle of waterless-wash antibacterial solution. It is available at all drugstores. On our most recent trip, three months in Southeast Asia, we carried this item for the first time. We were careful to use it, if we were unable to wash with soap, before eating anything. We can't be sure this precaution prevented digestive tract upheavals., but we were pleased that this trip was unusually healthy. We brought home almost all the Pepto-Bismol™ we took with us.

Remember too, toilet paper is a rare commodity in many developing country's public facilities. Keep a roll in your daypack.

Chapter Eight

HOW TO KEEP SIGHTSEEING COSTS LOW

FITs have already accomplished much in the way of traveling inexpensively by going on their own. They have not paid the hidden costs incurred by hiring someone to book their flights, choose and reserve a hotel, and plan their meals. When they arrive at their destination, they will only pay for what they want to do and see, based on their own interests and research. With experience, they will get the most out of their sightseeing budget.

Sightseeing—checking off a list of must sees established by tour guides, tourism departments and obliging writers of guidebooks—need not be a high priority of the frugal traveler. For one thing, a little sightseeing goes a long way. By your third pyramid, fourth mosque or fifth golden Buddha, you are no longer impressed. You just want something cold to drink and a shady place to sit down. Furthermore, memorable moments aren't as likely to happen when you are gawking at a famous landmark. They occur more often during the everyday events of living in this new place, i.e., during lunch at a small cafe, riding the bus, renting a room from a family, resting on a park bench, buying grapes from a vendor.

This is not to say you will intentionally ignore the Eiffel Tower if you are in Paris, or that you won't make an effort to get to Agra in India to see the Taj Mahal. Many world-renowned sights are well worth a visit, but you won't want to make them the whole point of your trip.

This is relevant to frugal travel because you can spend a lot of money sightseeing and not necessarily add value to your experience.

As an example, George and I may be among the few Americans to go to China and *not* see the Great Wall. We regret not seeing the Great Wall, but it didn't work out. It slipped lower and lower on our priority list as we traveled because so many other things came along to engage our attention and use up our time. Other travelers had told us about places in China they loved, and we saw them first. Sightseeing was only one small part of why we were in China, and the longer we were there, the less important it became.

The problem with making sightseeing the goal of a trip is that sightseeing is essentially passive. In a way, it's like watching a TV show about rafting the Colorado River through the Grand Canyon instead of doing it yourself and getting splashed with icy water in the rapids.

If you get on a tour bus, or hire a guide, and go from sight to sight, what do you have at the end but a few photos, maybe with you or your spouse standing in front of some famous pile of rock? Better to plan on visiting several small, French cathedral towns. Check out the cathedrals as you are moved to do so, but give the rest of the town some time as well. Wander the streets, have a drink in the cafes, admire the vegetable gardens. The cathedrals will fit into a whole. They will not be an end in themselves, but an aspect of your visit.

Participation Travel

The differences between being a passive sightseer and a more participating traveler became clearer to me after our second visit to Thailand. During our first visit, a four-day stop in Bangkok, we signed up for a guide and a car to show us the sights near the city. We paid $100 for a day of sightseeing, and not much value was added to our trip. Included in the tab was a canal boat ride, a visit to a tourist destination called the Rose Garden, and shopping for mementos.

Our driver took us to several shops where proprietors had chained hapless monkeys to trees as items of curiosity to be photographed. The shops were full of carved trinkets saying things about Thailand in English. We had no interest in buying any of this stuff, but made a loop through them to be polite while the shopkeepers followed us around hopefully.

The Rose Garden events were not much better. Lavishly costumed dancers performed ancient Thai rituals while a man with a buzzing microphone tried to explain them to a large, noisy and inattentive crowd. It reminded me of a circus, and seemed disrespectful of the Thai culture, rather than a celebration of it. Elephants paraded around giving rides, and handlers draped pythons around the necks of nervous-looking tourists for photo-ops.

Something bothered me about that day, but I didn't understand what it was until several years later when we came back for a longer visit to this friendly country.

On this second trip we had a lot more time and we were more experienced. We set out to explore on our own, to see what we could of life in Thailand.

We traveled by bus and commuter ferry to the island of Koh Samui. We stayed in a beach side cabin and ate at a variety of open-air restaurants dotting the beach. They showed American movies on video cassette every night. We rented a motorscooter to explore the island's Buddhist ruins, jungle waterfalls, and more remote beaches.

To the north, we discovered a Thailand less touched by the

95

modern world. We flew to the little mountain town of Mae Hong Son. The town is graced with a scenic temple on a lake. Every morning at dawn, saffron-robed monks, each carrying a bowl, emerged out of the mist. They walked in a line through town and people rushed out and put food in their bowls. This was a way of "making merit," we were told—getting points for heaven.

In Mae Hong Son we met a young British couple and together we hired a local guide named Pisit who was working his way through college by guiding for a tour company. He took us on a three day walk to visit villages accessible only by elephant or on foot. Unlike our previous guided trip, this time we were not going to places set up exclusively for tourists. Instead we were visitors to functioning tribal Thai communities. The only entertainment was simply to be there.

The first day we climbed a ladder up into a treehouse where a pipe-smoking grandmother shooed the chickens away and served us a meal of tea and noodles. Our guide interpreted as we asked her questions about her life in this place.

We spent the nights in huts on stilts in other villages, eating brown rice for dinner and again for breakfast. Our guide apologized for the rice, which the villagers did not have the means to polish. It was grown by our hosts, and hulled by them in a foot-powered device made of logs. The design had been around for centuries. "Peasant rice," said Pisit. We explained to him that we actually preferred brown rice, but he couldn't imagine we were serious.

On our last evening I pulled out the stash of balloons I had brought to give away. I thought I had enough to give one to every child in the village, but, as I blew them up and passed them out to wide-eyed, serious-faced, barefooted urchins, the word spread. More and more kids appeared and then the balloons were gone. It was interesting to see how readily the children who had balloons shared them with those who did not. Many of the children, Pisit told me, had never seen a balloon.

Visitors to underdeveloped countries may break the ice with local people if they bring small gifts. Ball-point pens are especially popular, but look around for other small items you can carry to give away.

On the way back to Mae Hong Son we rode elephants for one stretch. They were borrowed for us from their work of hauling timber. To show off their elephants' surefootedness, the handlers chose a steep path up a ridge. As we climbed, the little platform to which we clung swayed and dipped, rocked and lurched. The English woman quickly had enough of that, and insisted on being put down to walk behind us with Pisit the rest of the way.

This second journey to Thailand brought us into much more intimate contact with ordinary Thai people, not just those hired to entertain or sell to tourists. We were guests rather than circus patrons, and that was preferable.

The Taj Mahal

I wouldn't want to have missed seeing this world wonder. How impressive it was to touch its stone, walk on the marble floors, marvel at its design and symmetry, admire the artistically carved stone screens and the walls decorated with inlaid colored stone, and consider its 400 years as a monument to a man's love for a woman.

Nevertheless, my other memories of Agra are equally as important to me. The image of the Taj is indelible but what is also ingrained on my memory is the view from the backside of an ancient walled palace. We looked down a cliff onto a river lined with hundreds of women doing their laundry in the muddy water. Near them, boys drove water buffalo across the shallow, wide expanse. Perhaps a privileged princess once stood on this same spot, centuries ago, and saw the same scene.

The bicycle rickshaw wallahs of Agra taught us a lot about travel in India. They were particularly persistent at pestering tourists to hire them. What they really wanted to do was to take you to someone's shop because they would get a commission if you bought something. They were willing to wait while you ate lunch, saw the Taj, or even took a nap, for the opportunity to haul you somewhere to shop. George and I often walked to avoid being hassled to go shopping. Every 50 feet or so another rickshaw wallah would stop to ask if we wanted a ride. We explained we preferred to walk, and they reacted with anger. They could not understand why people with rupees in their pockets would walk, depriving a rickshaw wallah of his fee. Most of them, we learned, rented their rickshaws for eight rupees a day (about 50 cents). They could not afford to buy them at 2,000 rupees ($120).

One evening a rickshaw man insisted we ride for free with him to the restaurant to which we were walking. If we did, he told us, the restaurant owner would give him a cup of coffee. We ought to help him because he was a poor man, he told us.

We began to see a pattern here. Many Indian men (few women were engaged in commerce of any sort) seemed to believe tourists were obliged to accept and pay for whatever they were offering. One day at a fabric shop a clerk threw some tie-dyed cotton on the floor, stalked out the door and sat down in front of the shop to sulk when I told him I liked the cloth, but did not want to buy it.

We could see India's many beggars exhibited the same attitude. If they were out there with their hand out, clearly it was our duty to put something in it. When we did not, they were loud in their objections.

This fascinating self-righteousness would never have become so obvious to us if we hadn't been down in the streets with the people. In an air-conditioned tour bus, we would have missed out. India, we were discovering, was compelling for far more than her splendid monuments on must see lists.

In Jaipur, another beguiling, ancient Indian city, we saw astonishing forts and palaces, but the ordinary life of the city's residents was again more intriguing. Renting bicycles to get around was an experience in itself. Our hotel man directed us to a truck repair shop which rented bikes on the side. When we walked in, the proprietor asked us to sit down.

"Where are you going on the bicycles?" he asked.

We looked at each other. This was going to take time.

"Just around Jaipur," George said.

The man began a long discourse. He would like to rent us

bicycles, but he didn't know us, and what guarantee did he have that we would return the bikes at all, let alone in good condition? As he spoke, voicing his agony over the problem, he dipped fried *samosas* (bread pockets stuffed with spicy vegetables) into a cupped leaf full of yogurt.

George got the unspoken message. The man wanted money. He offered him a 1,000 rupee deposit—the large sum of $56. His face lit up. He reassured George that he did not have to worry about his money; it would be safe. He wrote a receipt. George signed it; he signed it. He stamped it.

But we weren't finished yet. Next we had to discuss the price per day we would pay for the bikes. We settled on five rupees a day—28 cents for each bike. Then he wanted to know exactly when we would be bringing them back—the day and time. We didn't have any idea, nor did we care to think about it at the moment, but we had no choice. We got out our pocket calendar and decided on 4 p.m. in three days. *Finally*, we were given the precious bicycles. They were in good shape except that the seats were too low and could not be raised. We pedaled off, shaking our heads.

There was so much to see on the streets of Jaipur, we could hardly concentrate on steering our bicycles through it all. The traffic was thick, but not with cars. We saw bullock carts. The white animals were painted with designs that looked as if they had been applied with red clay. Bright green stripes emphasized their horns.

Bicycle rickshaws crammed in four or five school boys wearing British-looking maroon blazers and navy pants. Camel carts, speedier than the bullock-drawn vehicles and loaded with sacks of grain or stacks of tires passed us. I loved watching the huge feet of the tall camels hit the pavement and splay out with a distinct squishing sound. I wondered if it hurt their feet, evolved for walking on soft sand.

Three-wheeled bus-taxis, each carrying twenty or so people and propelled by a tiny motorcycle engine, added to the noise. An occasional elephant lumbered along, his massive face decorated

99

with bright paint circling his eyes and pointing down his trunk.

Buses, bicycles and bicycle carts more or less completed the modes of transportation surrounding us.

No one was courteous, everyone honked and jangled, and chaos reined. Successful riding, we concluded, required equal measures of bravado, willingness to stand your ground, fast reflexes, a wary eye, some caution, and a quick hand on the brake.

In the evening we retreated to the quiet of our hotel—the former house of a maharajah. We had a room for $12 a night in what we surmised must have been the servants' quarters. In the library there were photos of the maharaja and his family. One, dated 1936, showed them receiving Lord Mountbatten and his wife at some occasion in this house. We were served tea in a spacious, breezy dining room on chipped china presumably left by the royal family.

India was not easy, but we'd like to go back. Not only to see more palaces, forts, cities and monuments, but to get caught up again in the pulse of life that beats so differently from our own.

Interactive Travel

One step up from participation travel is the kind that gets you so involved with the place that your presence there actually has an effect after you are gone. International Habitat for Humanity's house building projects are one example of this sort of organized do-good travel. There are many others.

Sometimes opportunities come along for an individual traveler to make a difference. When it happens, you can feel good about achieving truly interactive travel. The trick is to recognize your chances, and act on them when they present themselves. One such experience for me took place in China.

Not far from our hotel in Xian was a little sidewalk cafe called the Small World. The young man who ran it spoke excellent English. We asked him his name.

"My English name is William," he said.

"But what is your Chinese name?" we asked, thinking we should try to learn that instead.

"You won't remember it," he said with a smile.

"Oh, yes we will," I claimed.

So he told us, and I practiced saying it several times. The next day we came back for another meal.

"Hello . . ." I said, drawing a blank on his Chinese name. "Hello, William!"

"You see." he said. "Lots of my friends who work with foreigners take English names. It's easier."

Several restaurants we visited in China were beginning to offer meals familiar to Western visitors in addition to their Chinese dishes. Breakfast was a special challenge, since Chinese noodles seems like a peculiar way to start to the day to most foreigners. William's cafe had a dish on the lunch menu that we thought might have been good for breakfast, but he didn't serve it then. It was an egg and tomato combination. He made it for us one morning when we asked.

Later it occurred to me that I could help him learn to cook a simple, western-style breakfast. French toast, I thought. That would be easy and the ingredients should be readily available.

The next day I asked him if he would like me to teach him to make French toast, explaining what it was and what he needed to have on hand to make it. He was pleased with my offer, and we agreed to meet the next morning at 7:30. He had bought French bread, eggs, milk and a sweet apple butter sort of topping.

The only pans in the kitchen were woks, so I showed William and his helpers how to mix the batter, dip the bread, and fry it in a little oil one piece at a time in the bottom of a wok. George and I ate their first efforts, and they were quite acceptable.

Later that morning we passed the Small World on our way back to the hotel. William had put a large sign in the window: FRENCH TOAST FOR BREAKFAST. We stopped to see how things were going, and William was beaming.

"I have sold eleven French toasts," to told us.

There was a slice cooking at that moment. It was swimming in oil. The Chinese believe that the more oil you use, the more generous you are being to your guests.

101

"William," I said, "remember, and this is very important, only a little bit of oil just so the bread doesn't stick. Westerners don't like so much oil."

He asked if I would show him how to make pancakes next, but unfortunately we were leaving Xian later that day. I wrote down a recipe for him, but felt doubtful about his ability to make pancakes when he had had no experience with them. I suggested he ask another visitor for help, and I told him to buy a flat pan.

I haven't had a more meaningful or satisfying interactive travel experience. That small success has encouraged me to look for more opportunities, and has given me the courage to act on them as well.

Adventure Travel

Frugal travelers soon learn they need not pay a high price to have a memorable stay in a foreign country. Once you are on the scene, you can usually find local transportation and local people to guide you if you need guiding. You don't need to sign up for a tour at home, and pay American prices for developing-country experiences, or inflated prices for sightseeing you can purchase on location for much less—if you shop around.

The same thing is true when you seek adventure travel. It is a growing segment of the travel market. Adventure travel appeals to people who are looking for vacations more stimulating than restful. The trips involve a wide range of physical participation—from as active as bicycling or mountain climbing to as passive as clinging to a raft or bird watching.

I applaud the adventure travel trend. Better to be outdoors tramping around than riding a tour bus. At least it's likely to involve exercise. However, like most organized travel, adventure travel comes at a high price.

A recent ad in *Escape* magazine, for example, offers 15 days of sea kayaking, white water rafting and wilderness trekking in Indonesia for $1975, not including airfare. This amounts to a hefty $131 per day per person to sleep outdoors and eat camp food in a country where most people make $1 a day or less. It is reasonable to speculate that a person could travel much more cheaply, even if they *were* to rent a kayak.

For those who would never make it to Indonesia on their own, the $131 per day may be reasonable. But many Americans may not be aware that they can experience adventure travel, the same as more ordinary travel, for considerably less cost. The key is in knowing that specific plans can be made after you arrive in the destination country, using local resources to accomplish your adventure.

There are caveats, of course. Besides the fact that making your own arrangements takes extra time, the trip you put together yourself may lack frills, amenities, and comforts. You may have glitches and disappointments. You need to be cautious about whom you hire. Most people are trustworthy, but we have heard tales about dishonest folks who run off with peoples' cameras or luggage. Locally hired guides and porters probably won't speak English, so you will have to work harder to gain an understanding about the place you are visiting.

Nevertheless, the cost differential can be stunning. It may mean, for some people, the difference between going on a travel adventure and staying at home hoping to win a lottery. Or the difference between having seven adventures or having only one.

In our experience, many adventures packaged and sold in the U.S. for $100 and more a day (plus international airfare) can be bought locally for pennies on the dollar. Furthermore, these do-it-yourself adventures offer several advantages in addition to cost savings. They are good for the countries you are visiting because the money goes wholly to local people—many of them extremely needy. Another important issue: depending on the activity, you may make less of a demand on the environment with your more modest requirements compared to the pampered tour-adventure traveler. Finally, self-directed adventure travel guarantees more contact with local people, and this will result in a more interesting trip.

George and I have not tested our theories about frugal adventure travel on every continent, but we believe it is safe to wager that local options exist wherever international adventure travel companies have set up operations. For those who have the time and are willing to make the effort, low-cost adventures await you. No reservations required.

Trekking in Nepal

We encountered the best example of the ease and low cost of making your own adventure in Nepal. For years we had talked about our hope of one day walking among the magnificent peaks of the Himalayas. We had no ambition to be mountaineers and join an expedition to scale any of these monsters. We just wanted to see for ourselves the Earth's most vaulted heights—to have a good, close look. We organized our year of frugal travel so we would arrive in Nepal in November, the ideal trekking month. The monsoon is over and the cold is not yet severe.

We flew to Katmandu from Bangkok on a flight we arranged just two weeks ahead of time. When we landed, we found a cheap guesthouse and picked up a tourist paper published in English. Many local trekking companies advertised in the paper and our guidebook recommended hiring a porter and/or a guide through a trekking company. It was possible to find young men offering their services at the trail heads. Although hiring off the trail was cheaper, it was more risky. The trekking companies guarantee the trustworthiness of the people they hire.

We interviewed several companies, all of which had English-speaking personnel. We decided to take the 150-mile Annapurna loop trail, a frequently used trade route as well as a popular trek, so we did not need a guide. A porter to help us carry our gear, however, would be a welcome luxury. We picked a company offering a porter for $5 a day. On top of that, we would have to pay him up to $2.50 a day for his living expenses (a bed in a lodge and meals). Another $10 a day should cover our living expenses, we were told. Figuring in the cost of the trekking permit and transportation to and from Katmandu, the trek would cost around $20 to $25 a day for both of us. This was in 1988. At the time the adventure travel companies were charging American tourists $100 a day *each*, for the same walk.

Our month-long trek was everything we hoped it would be and more. We set off with Krishna, our 19-year-old porter (who spoke almost no English), at a rice-growing elevation. We watched people harvest the grain by hand as we walked along using an umbrella to ward off the intense sun. Gradually the trail climbed, the snowy peaks in the distance edged closer, and the temperature dropped.

The trail was busy with commerce. Many European climbing expeditions mingled with caravans of ponies and burros wearing plumed headdresses made of yak tail wool, dyed red, and festooned with jangling bells. They were carrying supplies for the many villages along the route.

Goods were carried by humans as well. Most used large baskets with a leather strap securing the load to their foreheads. My neck ached to look at them. We couldn't get over the weight these tiny people carried, most of them while wearing only rubber thongs on their blackened and callused feet. One man had six cases of soft drinks in glass bottles roped together on his back.

Tea stalls along the way offered outdoor rock bench seats so that porters could sit down and rest their loads without taking them off their backs. They would congregate at these places, chatting and laughing as they took a break. They were friendly, and we bought our tea and sat among them, enjoying the warmth of the intense, high-altitude sunshine.

In the afternoon, we would stop early if we came across a village that seemed particularly pleasant, or a lodge offering a nice room. The villages were primitive. Most had no running water, though a few had locally generated hydroelectric power. Water came from the town pump, and occasionally we were given a bucket of hot water for washing, but not often. Fuel for heating water was too scarce. Dense forests have vanished in Nepal with the demands for timber. (A few years later I met an American who raved about his wonderful adventure tour trek in Nepal. He had a hot bath every night, he said. I thought about all the porters carrying wood, and another carrying a bathtub just so this group on their "adventure" could have a luxury denied everyone else around them.)

The villages, particularly as we climbed to those dominated by Buddhists, were festooned with prayer flags. The stone houses had carved window frames, and the flat roofs were stacked with bundles of hay for winter. Stone inscription walls and prayer wheels lined the paths. The rooms we rented were small and simple, with two narrow beds, a candle or a kerosene lamp, and, if we were lucky, a few nails in the wall on which to hang our jackets. Most came with a glassless window with shutters against the cold. None had any heat beyond the cooking fireplace in the common room. As we gained elevation, we went to bed earlier and earlier in order to crawl into the warmth of our sleeping bags.

We ate in the family common room, an open area with a firepit, stools, and sometimes tables and chairs. Twice in the coldest towns we stayed in places where a large table was built in a pit. Benches lined the edges, and a heavy cloth covered the table and the visitors' legs. Under the table the proprietor would put a precious bucket of hot coals. Trekkers would sit for hours at these tables, long after the meal was finished, writing, reading, socializing and staying warm. They were international tables, but often the conversation would be conducted in English, the language most had in common.

The Nepali people were reserved but welcoming. They are physically small, sturdy, thin, handsome and hard-working. The women often fed large numbers of guests, cooking huge vats of rice for the usual dinner of *dahl baht* (rice with a smattering of lentils and potatoes.)

I remember one woman in particular. She was pretty, with long black hair tied in a bun. She wore the usual necklace of a strand of coral and turquoise stones, and earrings made of strings of tiny white shells. She held a tiny baby in her left arm as she cooked with her right. From time to time she adjusted her brown, woolen dress so the child could nurse.

The bright-eyed, rosy-cheeked children were adorable. My fingers itched to soothe their chapped faces with some rich, protective lotion. If we go again, I'll bring small tubes as gifts.

The hiking was hard, but we got progressively tougher. I enjoyed the river crossings on swinging footbridges, racing ahead to photograph those behind me. What I didn't like was hand-washing clothes in cold water with powdered detergent that didn't dissolve well. Particularly gruesome was washing bandanas. Toilet paper and tissue were so scarce we didn't want to waste any blowing our frequently runny noses, so we used bandanas. In desperation I tried to learn the male-trail method of nose clearing—aim away from your feet and expel air forcefully through one nostril at a time. I was not proficient yet when one day I tried this while sitting on a bench outside a tea stall. George was sitting next to me wearing shorts. I missed the ground and hit his bare thigh. Krishna looked at George and me with fear on his face. What would George do?

"Good shooting!" George said to me. We started to laugh. Krishna looked uncertain, but then joined in. The three of us were overcome by cathartic guffaws for some minutes.

"Good shooting," Krishna would repeat, and we would be off again.

At the trail's maximum elevation we crossed Thorong La, an 18,000 foot pass surrounded by the Annapurna peaks which towered 26,000 feet. We took some pride in walking over this pass when several much younger trekkers had to turn back with altitude sickness.

The scenery was worth the effort. Evenings, I would sit and stare at the peaks, looking with field glasses at the blocks of ice as big as houses littering the surface of glaciers. I saw plumes of snow blow into the sky as winds howled about the summits, while here below only a gentle breeze blew.

By candlelight at night we were reading books about historic climbs in the Himalayas. I would shiver to look at a peak like Dhaulagiri and think about the American team that had been wiped out by an avalanche in 1959 trying to be the first to make the top of that formidable mountain.

We had many other memorable moments . . .

107

- Bathing in a river with village children who begged shampoo from me. We all lathered up together.
- The time we spent bargaining with an old man dressed in woolen robes and wearing strings of turquoise. He was selling a tiny perfume vial to be worn around the neck.
- Lying awake one night because a healer had been hired to chant outside our house to cure a sick child.
- Soaking in hot springs in the village of Totopani. The village was slowly slipping into the river from erosion.
- In the same village, we ate homemade apple tarts baked by a woman who met her husband for the first time on the day they celebrated their arranged marriage.

When our trek was all over we took Krishna out for dinner in Pokara, gave him a tip, bought him a bus ticket, and started him off on his journey home. He would have to walk four days more after he got to Katmandu, but such a walk would take tourists like us at least eight days, he asserted. He was convinced Nepalis were the strongest walkers in the world. He bid us a tearful farewell and said when we came back we had only to ask for him, and he would take us on another trek.

We hope to do just that.

Chapter Nine

SECURITY WHEN TRAVELING FRUGALLY

We got on the Lisbon Metro in mid-afternoon, well before rush hour. Suddenly a crushing crowd surrounded us as we found a spot to stand near the door. Up to that point we had not been particularly wary in Portugal. After all, we'd traveled in cities with worse reputations. George spoke to me urgently.

"Watch your camera," he said. "Something funny is going on."

I looked down at my camera, hung over my shoulder by a strap. The flap was open, and the camera was half out of the bag!

I looked at the man pressed against my side. He was looking straight ahead, only inches from me. Could he have been trying to steal it? I shoved the camera back in its bag and moved it around so I could clutch it to my chest.

The train pulled into the next station. It wasn't our stop, but George said, "Let's get out of here."

We fought our way to the door and burst out in relief.

"Did you lose anything?" he asked.

I took off my day pack. The zipper had been opened, but nothing was missing. I knew better than to carry valuables there.

"No, but that man almost got my camera. Do you think they were all working together?"

"Yes. No one was near, then we were surrounded. Uh oh."

"What?"

"Our bus tickets to the Algarve are gone."

"Oh, no. Where were they?"

"In my back pocket. I put them there after we bought them. I didn't feel nervous here, but it looks as if I should have."

"We'll buy more. At least it was only $20."

It happens, even to those of us who should know better, but it happens a *lot* to people who are unprepared. Thieves and pickpockets the world over prey on travelers. Frugal travelers, using local transportation and staying in small hotels in less than fancy neighborhoods, are especially vulnerable. However, simple precautions and awareness can protect you. With all our tramping around in the world, we've only been robbed twice. Once in Portugal, as described, and once in Lima. In both cases our own carelessness was to blame.

In Lima, it was our last night. We changed just enough money to get through the evening and pay for a late night taxi to the airport. We stopped at a liquor store on the way back to our hotel to buy a bottle of local rum to take home. George put the change in his right front pants pocket. (We know—you shouldn't ever put money in your pants pockets.) He was holding the bottle with his right hand, and he had his left arm around me. We were feeling so happy. After four great months in South America, we were heading home. Suddenly, we both stumbled, and almost fell; someone had careened into us with menacing force.

"What was that?" I asked, surprised and distressed. I turned and watched a man racing away from us down the sidewalk.

"A pickpocket," George said. "He got my money."

"You're kidding! I thought pickpockets were sneaky, not like linebackers."

"Now we know," he said. "He just rammed his hand in my pocket as he was pushing me."

We sat in our hotel room puzzling over what had happened. We had only lost the equivalent of about $8, but we were still upset. We had been so careful, and to get robbed on our last night in South America was pretty humiliating. We figured the thief must have watched us change money on the square, then followed us to the liquor store. Usually any cash we had went into pouches around our necks or in George's shirt pocket. This one time, for the two minute walk to our hotel, he put it in his pants.

Now, years later, we are over being mad, and hope the man was able to make good use of the money. Perhaps he was desperately poor, and stealing to feed his family. The inequities of the world cannot be ignored forever.

The world shows us two faces when we travel. The first is a smiling, friendly, welcoming, honest and respectful face. People help us, invite us into their homes, make room for us on buses and trains, share tables with us in crowded restaurants, and generously show us who they are and what they do. If they feel resentment because we are North Americans with money and leisure to travel, it is rarely obvious.

A more sinister face exists, however. This face is worn by those who, no doubt, are desperately poor, and see travelers of any nationality as rich targets. So rich that, as the thief probably sees it, we won't miss a little of our wealth if he helps himself to some of it. Many of us must look like loaded berry bushes, with purses, cameras, leather bags, daypacks, neck pouches and waist pouches dangling from us like ripe fruit ready for plucking—usually without thorns.

A favorite topic of conversation among travelers are tales of rip-offs they've heard of or experienced. Such stories have been repeated often and perhaps embellished in the retelling, but we have heard enough to know some creative scoundrels are out there. The cautionary stories are worth relating here. They provided information that has helped us protect ourselves—to grow a few thorns and make the job of the fruit pluckers a little tougher. We can spare some of our riches, but we would rather be the ones to make the decision about what to give. Moreover, we would rather give money or gifts in exchange for services rendered, to people who have earned them.

Some of these tales may be depressing. It is sad to acknowledge that many people would steal from us, and will do so, if we give them half a chance. Nevertheless, take this information in stride and don't let it frighten you into staying home. Instead, fortify yourself with cautious optimism.

Believe most everyone you encounter will be friendly and honest, but do what you can to avoid being victimized by those who are not. Accept this facet of travel as one more challenge to be dealt with, and get on with your trip. Understand that these thieves are only doing a job—it's nothing personal. Like the beggars in India, they have created a street profession. This is what they do to survive. We don't like it, and we don't have to cooperate, but we believe most of them mean us no harm.

Few tourists are physically hurt by these thieves, but every year many thousands do lose valuables through their own failure to protect themselves.

Simple Precautions

✔ Leave valuable trinkets and jewelry at home. You may be crazy about, and never take off, the diamond pendant your sweetie gave you for Valentine's Day, but how would you like to have it torn off your neck as you walk down the street? We've heard of this and worse, such as earrings being pulled out of pierced earlobes.

We wear sturdy, inexpensive watches, and I skip jewelry unless it's local *artesania* I've just purchased. Hand-painted beads from a nearby mountain town don't interest thieves.

✔ Flashy dress, particularly in countries with a large population of poor people, doesn't make good sense. This is generally not a problem for us *mochileros*. We cannot fit silk cocktail dresses into our packs anyway. Dressing up for us means wearing a colorful sash or silk scarf with our black knit skirt and cleanest T-shirt, which is probably for the best.

✔ Leave purses and wallets at home. This is a difficult notion for some people to accept. We women are so attached to our purses, we feel naked without them. Where will I carry my hairbrush, I wondered, as we planned our earliest adventures? What about my reading glasses? Lip gloss? Notebook? Pens?

Men, too, feel at a loss when told they can't have their wallets. What do you do with IDs, credit cards, money, phone cards, ATM cards?

Wallets and purses are so easy to steal, I cannot urge you strongly enough to leave them behind. In a moment I'll tell you how to cope.

✔ *Never carry money in your pants pockets*. We were waiting for a bus once in Cochabamba, Bolivia. As I climbed on behind George, I noticed the back pocket of his jeans gaping open.

Someone had neatly sliced it down the middle, probably with a razor, as we waited in the crowd for the bus. George hadn't even noticed. The thief had made off with a flattened roll of toilet paper he had been carrying there.

✔ Never carry anything valuable in a daypack. We have heard dozens of stories—many of them heartbreakers—about travelers being separated from their daypacks. The packs had, regrettably, often functioned as purse and wallet substitutes. Travelers' checks, airplane tickets, cash, and even passports disappeared. One tearful English girl in Jaipur, India, had lost all of the above when her daypack vanished while she was eating lunch. She had it hung on the back of her chair.

Use daypacks to carry things you need to have readily accessible i.e., hairbrush, glasses, sunscreen, guidebooks and maps, a journal, postcards to write, pens, toilet paper, a snack, a bandana, a camp knife for peeling fruit, a water bottle, and soap for hand washing. Although most of these items are replaceable, we still don't want to lose them, so we have a strategy. Whenever we take off a daypack in a public place, we hold it in our laps, or set it down on a chair next to us where we can either watch it or hook it through one arm. Or we put it on the floor with a leg through the strap. Be sure and hand it to your traveling buddy if you are going to leave it behind to go to a restroom. Do not put it in overhead bins on buses or trains. Keep it cozily near you.

When we feel particularly nervous, we protect daypacks from being opened and pilfered by wearing them on our chests instead of our backs. We also wear them this way when carrying our large backpacks, instead of fastening them to the outside of the backpack or carrying them in our hands where we might inadvertently set them down.

In a bus station in Oaxaca, Mexico, I left George in charge of our large backpacks and two daypacks while I tried to find out what was delaying our departure. A man came and sat down next to George and began to speak to him. George was suspicious. A second man sat down in the row of seats behind George at about the same time, facing the opposite way. George looked at him just as he snaked his hand over the row of chairs and down toward one of the day packs. Of course, Geo had a good grip on the packs, but he spoke to both men, suggesting something about "buzzing off."

✔ Be suspicious of any distraction. The one man trying to divert George's attention so another could grab a day pack is a common trick, as is the one we encountered in Lisbon when we lost our bus tickets. We had also heard tales about the team-with-mustard trick while we were in South America; when it happened to me in Cuzco, I was ready for it. Someone bumps into you, "accidentally" spilling something gross on you. After the spill, the offender tries to stop you, if you are walking, to help you wipe it off, miraculously having a rag handy. If you are in a restaurant, the perpetrator tries to lead you off to the restroom to clean you up, leaving your belongings behind for the co-conspirators to grab and run.

In Cuzco, a tiny old woman somehow got this yellow stuff that smelled like detergent all over my shoulder as I was walking through a marketplace.

"Uh oh," I thought, and kept on walking. The market wasn't crowded, but suddenly I was surrounded. A small boy on my right was tugging at the camera strap slung over my shoulder. I grabbed the camera bag with my right hand, stopped and twisted my body right and left as though ridding myself of entanglements—which I was—and began to walk energetically and as fast as I could. The crowd fell back. I still had everything, though my daypack zipper was hanging open, my shirt was a mess, and my heart was pounding from the adrenaline rush.

✔ What your mother always said was true—never take candy from strangers. In Thailand, we heard of more than one case where someone on a bus ride was offered something to eat by a friendly stranger, then passed out and was robbed. We actually met someone to whom this had happened. She was a young German who ate a doped cookie. When she fell asleep, her companion did not know she had been drugged. Fortunately, he had not eaten any of the cookie, and kept track of their belongings all night as a matter of course. In the morning when the bus arrived at its destination, he could not wake her up. An ambulance took her to a hospital where she did wake up, some hours later, none the worse for her experience. The hospital did not tell her what she had been given.

✔ Carry your passport separately from your travelers checks. It surprised us to learn that stolen travelers checks are not always replaced. A young man traveling in South America had his day pack taken while on a bus. He knew his travelers' checks and passport were gone, but he waited to report the loss for a couple of days until he got to a city. By then, the thief had cashed the checks, using the passport number as verification, and the issuing bank refused to reimburse his loss. This may not always happen. However, you must be as careful with travelers' checks as you are with cash. Report their loss immediately.

✔ Always make duplicate photocopies of your valuables and carry them separately. I leave a third set of copies of my passport and various cards with my mother back home. List the numbers you need to call to report stolen cards in your portable address book.

How to Carry Valuables

Many travel advisers urge us to put our airplane tickets, excess cash and travelers checks in hotel safes. Good advice if only our frugal travel style hotels had safes but most do not. Generally, we are on our own in protecting our goods.

The best strategy is always to carry your irreplaceable valuables hidden on your person. Several options are available. Luggage/travel/recreation stores sell waist pouches in various sizes. You wear them outside your clothes and they are great for carrying some portion of your valuables. They also sell small, flat cloth money belts that you wear under your clothes. Shoulder, neck, waist and leg pouches are available, too. You may need more than one. Buy a variety, fill them up, and walk around with them. Take what is comfortable and works for you.

NOTE: A list of stores with a variety of travel goods for sale, including the above items, is listed in the Appendix.

The drawback is accessibility. How do you get at your money, your passport? What we do is each carry a small amount of cash in a safe but handy place, such as the exterior waist pouch. In South America we carried flat, embroidered bags around our necks. Actually coca pouches, these are worn by men in Bolivia and Peru engaged in heavy physical labor who like to have a nip handy to relieve hunger, thirst and fatigue with a chew. Travelers wear them to feel as if they are with it—part of the local scene.

Second, we have a pouch we can easily pull out from beneath our clothes. The pouch might contain the travelers' check we want to change that day, or a few larger bills of the local currency, a credit card, and an ATM card. We carry our passports only if we know we will have to produce them to register for a hotel room or leave the country. This pouch might be around the neck and under the shirt, or around the waist and tucked under the pants. The pouches are inconspicuous and inaccessible to the casual sneak-thief, the pocket-slitter thief, or even the hit-and-run linebacker pickpocket.

If you don't like the cord around your waist, you can try my modification. I sew two buttonholes in each of the pouches we dangle from our waists. Then I sew two buttons inside the waistbands of my two pairs of pants, my shorts, and skirt that I will be taking on the trip. I can flip these pouches up if I need to get into them; otherwise they hang there and don't bother me. Our other valuables—those for which we have no immediate need—we carry in yet another pouch that stays hidden on our bodies.

This third repository could be a leg pouch or a shoulder harness. In them, we stash travelers checks, cash, passports and airplane tickets. If anyone demands money, chances are we can give away the pouches hanging from our sides and neglect to mention that we have yet another stash.

Why all this secrecy? If we had only been carrying travelers' checks, we might not have taken this extra precaution. However, in developing countries, it is often beneficial to come with cash. A $100 bill is much more negotiable than a travelers' check in some countries, particularly when there is an active street market in money changing. Regardless, I do not recommend changing money on the street. The risks include being jailed for breaking local laws, or getting ripped off by fast-fingered professionals.

These days, with wide spread availability of ATMs around the world, the best rate of exchange is often the international bank rate available at these machines. Carrying cash is becoming less necessary. Use the above precautions to protect your plastic cards.

What about the Beach?

When our trips include the seashore, as they often do, we are faced with the dilemma of what to do with our valuables if we want to go swimming or snorkeling. We are not inclined to leave them wrapped in a pair of pants on a beach towel.

Several possibilities—team up with other travelers on the beach and take turns watching each other's stuff. This, of course, requires you know the others well enough to trust them. Another is to take turns going into the water with your traveling partner—if you have one.

The best, though, may be to purchase a waterproof pouch to use on such occasions. One that can hold passports, a ticket and travelers' checks should be large enough. Check them out at your local outdoor store or in the catalogs. Magellan's Travel Store in Santa Barbara, California is a great one. (See Appendix.)

Taking Care of a Camera

Carry a small, automatic camera in a daypack, using the recommended precautions with daypacks, and you should be safe. Heavier, more valuable and fragile cameras with interchangeable lenses are another problem.

I don't leave my camera equipment in hotel rooms, and it is a burden to be dragging it around with me all the time on backpacking trips to developing countries. However, I do it anyway. I carry it in its own sturdy shoulder bag. I used to take only one lens, a zoom from 28mm to 200. Then I bought a very light-weight camera and could upgrade to two new—and also light-weight lenses—a 28 to 75mm and an 80 to 300mm.

I keep a hawkeye on it if it is away from my body. In countries where I feel secure I may put it in an overhead bus or train rack.

117

On an overnight trip, I sleep with it over my shoulder and on my lap. Thieves are hot for cameras. Be alert and careful if you don't want to lose a valuable and important piece of trip equipment.

Frugal travel would certainly be simpler without the burden of a camera. Each person must decide what having that camera along is worth. For me, the camera adds to the trip a dimension I enjoy. I want to capture, as artfully as I can, the visual uniqueness of a place. On trips, I am constantly engaged in figuring out how to best do that.

Other Thievery

Thieves aren't all of the snatching variety. Some try to rob travelers by overcharging. Time after time we have had to relearn this lesson—discuss the price first and make sure everyone clearly understands the arrangement.

Never assume you know the price without asking. In Srinagar, Kashmir, our houseboat keeper arranged a trip for us in one of the lovely boats, called *shakaras*, that cruise Dal Lake. We had seen the prices posted on the town dock for such excursions, and we *assumed* that was the price we would be expected to pay.

The slow-paced trip lasted several hours with two or three stops. At one point among the lotus blossoms our paddler smoked a water pipe and took a nap, after asking us if we would mind if he took a short break. We finally woke him up and said we wanted to get back. When he dropped us at the houseboat, he asked for five times the going rate. We objected, and there was a heated discussion.

It's natural to assume no one would want to overcharge you, to avoid discussing money, and to pay whatever is asked. This is risky for the frugal traveler who is watching expenses carefully. Foreigners in many countries are regarded as rich targets by pickpockets and purse snatchers. They are also seen as easy marks by those hoping to sell overpriced goods and services.

While it may be fairly painless to give a poor bicycle rickshaw driver more than the going rate for his efforts, it also creates the impression among such drivers that tourists have so much money they don't care if they are being overcharged—or else they are too dumb to object. Frugal travelers suffer from such practices. We don't appreciate paying more than is normal.

Because of language barriers we keep a notepad and pen handy. If we aren't sure we have understood the asking price, we write the numbers down and show them to the driver. If he nods in agreement, we know we're clear. This works in a multitude of situations, from buying street food to securing a hotel room.

Buying street food makes a traveler particularly vulnerable. Someone offers you a tempting treat, such as skewered, marinated, broiled chicken on a bamboo stick. If you take a bite before asking the price, you are not in a very good position to argue if you think you are being overcharged.

It helps to get an idea of local prices before getting involved in any situation where the prices aren't clear. We find walking through open air markets or restaurants and listening to the prices being discussed is the best way of getting educated. If we know the going rate for skewered chicken is *wu mao*, then that is what we will be prepared to offer to pay as well.

Getting into any mode of conveyance makes us vulnerable as well. Sometimes if it's late and we're tired, we're so grateful at the prospect of a ride we think we won't mind paying just about anything. How much can a bicycle rickshaw driver charge, anyway? We have been amazed at what they will request, as they unload us at our destination. If we haven't settled on a fee before piling in, we don't have much choice but to pay—even if the price is way out of line.

In some countries overcharging foreigners is so common no one thinks of doing anything else. In such places the frugal traveler has to work long and hard to be treated like an ordinary citizen. In China, for example, there is one price for locals and another for tourists. We bought a slice of watermelon right after a local person did from a street vendor. We listened to the price and watched the transaction. When we asked for a piece, the price quoted was three times as high. We objected, offering the local rate. The vendor agreed only reluctantly to the lower price. He acted as though he was doing us a real favor.

It gets tiresome, always having to discuss he price before

doing anything. However, whenever we have gotten lax and failed to take this step, we have regretted it.

Bargaining

There are those who argue that those of us from developed countries, visiting the less developed, should be ashamed of ourselves for trying to knock a dollar or two—or even a quarter—off the price of an artifact or an apple from a street vendor who will never in her lifetime see the kind of money most Americans take home in a year. Such admonishment strikes guilt into the hearts of bargain-hunting travelers. It's true, we blush. What can we be thinking of? We should pay a generous price, whatever is asked, or why not even offer more? We could do our bit for income redistribution on a global scale.

The frugal traveler has a couple of problems with this guilt. While many of us would love to be generous, few travelers on a budget can afford it. If we are going to bring home any mementos, we have to carefully husband our resources. Inevitably, I like to gather much more than I can pay for. I will bargain fiercely with a vendor if I think by doing so I can buy two and have one to keep and one to give away.

Remember, no one is forcing a vendor to sell anything. If they don't think they are getting a fair offer, they can simply refuse to part with their goods.

Furthermore, in many countries, haggling over prices is so much a part of the culture we are considered fools if we simply pay the first price asked. In developing countries, the vendor expects to get what the market will bear, and no more. Travelers who pay what is asked without a blink make things tougher for those who come behind—travelers rich and poor.

Bargaining does not come easy to Americans. They are simply not used to it. But it is a skill the successful frugal traveler needs to develop.

It does not take long to understand the local customs in this regard. If we are quoted a price for a taxi ride and we object and offer less, and the driver agrees, we know that is how it's done. If, however, he shrugs and leaves us to shuffle off on our own two feet, we have also learned something. Either it's a seller's market, or rides aren't negotiable in this country.

The more you do it, the easier it gets. Bargaining goes best if you offer something in exchange for the lower price. "I can't pay that much for one. Can I pay 40 *baht* and get two?" "We can't pay that much for a room. Do you have a smaller one that costs less?" "That rate per hour is high. Can we keep the bicycles overnight if we pay for six hours?"

We have done so much bargaining on our travels I now do it sometimes at home. "These cherries are looking a little sad. Will you mark them down?" It's surprising how many prices are negotiable. I haven't had any luck with my dentist though, and I've tried.

Bargaining, by itself, is no guarantee of a fair price. In Chile we were charged twice the going rate for a taxi ride to a distant spa, even though we got the trip for half what he asked originally. We hadn't tried to find out ahead of time from a disinterested person what a reasonable fare would be.

We do much better at bargaining when we are armed with information. We talk to our hotelkeeper, other travelers, the tourist office staff. What should a taxi ride to this place cost? What do you pay for apples on the street? What is the value of a hand-knitted sweater? As is usually the case, ask for help and you will get it. Don't hesitate to ask.

Chapter Ten
CAN I GO HOME AGAIN?

According to a report from the World Bank in 1994, one billion people on this planet live on $1 a day or less. Isolated as we are in the United States from the impact of this fact, we can easily ignore it. However, we may be doing so at great risk to future peace and tranquillity. The more of us who undertake travel to developing countries, the more likely some awareness of the disparities that exist will penetrate our national consciousness.

The task facing the developed countries of the world at the moment, whether we recognize it or not, is to make good on the perceived promises of capitalism—still in the process around the world of philosophically triumphing over communism—to improve the quality of life for humankind. Without generosity by nations who are farther along on the road to economic prosperity, the capitalistic revolution, such as it is, could falter. Chaos and cold (or hot) war could return.

Not to make too big of a deal out of the importance of frugal travelers as contributors to world peace—but there is no doubt that traveling in countries where some of those one billion people are living hand-to-mouth does change you irrevocably. Frugal travel puts faces on those numbers.

I hear about refugees from Tibet living for years in exile in north India. I remember the beautiful Tibetan women bent over carrying rocks in cloth slings on their backs on a gompa construction site near Leh, Ladakh.

I read about political unrest in Bolivia. I think of the woman selling little piles of pink, yellow and purple potatoes from a cloth spread on a sidewalk in La Paz while her two small children entertained themselves as best they could on the cold pavement nearby.

I see a report about the demise of the Shining Path in Peru. I hope a reason to believe life will improve will come for the boys who beg passengers to throw money and food to them off passing trains.

Your faces will be different. You may not collect any at all, at first. Your initial frugal trip might be to a developed, or moderately developed country where people are not struggling so hard just to live. But once you open the door to FITness, you will be emboldened to be more adventurous, to step farther away from what is known and familiar, and into what is, for you, uncharted territory.

Wherever you go, it's worthwhile. Just as no education is wasted, no travel fails to change you—at least not if you are open to the experience, and aware of what is there to absorb.

I want to make one last important point about frugal travel. It's your trip, and you don't have to compare it to anybody else's.

There are those who urge us to travel independently not so much because it costs less, but because it leads us "off the beaten path." I argue the notion that we must abandon well trodden paths to be successful FITs is nonsense. Americans are competitive. Some people (not only Americans) are chartering airplanes to touch down on some atoll only to be able to say they've been there. They are counting countries for a life total, like some people count birds. Let's call this what it is—absurd.

Others, some of them frugal travelers, play a one-upmanship game. They are not satisfied to have been to Thailand, or even to have trekked to some remote villages. They have to have been invited to live in the village and then urged to marry the chieftain's daughter. I think the danger of getting caught up in these games is that, if you do, you fail to value what you have accomplished.

Nothing is wrong with following your guidebook and staying in the hostels or hotels recommended, or hunting up restaurants the author found to be a good value. Sure, it's fun to find your own neat places to stay and eat, but you don't have to do it to have a marvelous and even meaningful experience.

You don't have to be "off the beaten path." What's wrong with paths? I rather like well-worn paths leading to interesting places. Along them, we have met some marvelous fellow frugal travelers whom we have enjoyed for hours, days or weeks as we've traveled. A few have become friends, and these friendships have grown and nurtured all of us for years and years.

Those who urge us to follow their lead and go off the beaten path are really encouraging us to seek out an authentic experience. This is what the goal of any independent traveler should be. They are right to imply that if you go to Thailand and do nothing but visit the Rose Garden tourist extravaganza and buy trinkets in the shops along the way, you will not have tasted much of the real Thailand. The true advantage of independent frugal travel is that you soon learn the difference between authentic and canned or fake experience. Eventually, you want nothing to do with the fake, which is why we are exhorted by travel writers to leave the "beaten path" where authentic experience is a little tougher to come by.

I have a friend, a skilled FIT, who says he thinks people should take guidebooks like the *Lonely Planet* series, circle all the places recommended and avoid them like the plague. "Go everywhere *but* there," he says. He, and other experienced FITs, want to avoid what one writer has called the "pancake circuit" (backpacker restaurants and hotels around the world that cater to the needs and tastes of the independent, frugal traveler) because they believe authentic experience in such places has been lost. Globalization has overwhelmed the local culture. You'll hear American music, watch American movies, eat pancakes topped with yogurt and speak English to fellow travelers. How can you experience the country you are visiting?

I don't agree. I love the backpacker circuit for the companion-ship of other travelers, the information exchanged, and the comfort of familiar food and nice lodgings at low prices. How-ever, be aware that being in such an environment does insulate you from the realities of the country where you are. If you can use the backpacker havens as a retreat when you've had enough nitty gritty exposure to the rest of the country, you'll not lose out on the authentic experiences you want.

Authentic experience can be as simple as riding one of those Indian video buses with the awful, sexist movies or as terrific as having a Himalayan journey with Jogmohinder in his Tata. It can be as sublime as the amazing time I had in Ladakh and feel so grateful for now. Several of us hired a taxi from Leh to ride to the little village of Tak-Tak. An enterprising backpacker had learned a religious festival was to he held there that day, and they did not mind if tourists came to watch.

In the village, the main ceremonial building had a roofed pavilion off to one side. Spectators arranged themselves on plank benches in rows on two sides. A troop of monks including several small boys came out of the *gompa* making music with cymbals, drums and long, brass horns. It was magical; something out of *National Geographic*—and I was there.

For the next several hours, characters in elaborate masks and costumes came out and danced. We Westerners could not fathom much of what it all meant, but we did grasp the importance of the occasion to the local people who were dressed in their finest woolen robes, jewelry and goat skin wraps, and who gave the ceremonies their rapt attention. We felt so privileged to be there.

The world is changing rapidly; soon all this marvelous diversity will have eroded away. It's worth the effort to go looking for it while it still exists.

Measure your success in achieving authentic travel experience against your own personal standards. Keep those standards flexible. You may start out thinking you are going to spend two months in China, but if you get one of the common respiratory problems that make people sick (all that coal burning pollutes the air), you may have to give up and go home early. Don't look at it as defeat. You were in China, you learned a lot, and you gave it your best shot.

Frugal travel can get you down. Some days, when I miss talking to my children, feel guilty about leaving my mother, or long to be in my own kitchen with a real oven, I wonder if I am I

126

crazy to be chasing around the world, living poor, sometimes getting sick, working so hard to keep within a budget? Maybe we should just stay home and let the icemaker keep us in cold, pure drinks. Stay home, where both of us can drive our own personal automobile whenever and wherever we choose—something unheard of in many places in the world.

After a little reflection, the answer is always "no." Our travel experiences have given us a priceless gift—an awareness of, and a connection to, some of the other humans who inhabit the Earth. We gained a perspective on their lives, and on our own, we could not have obtained any other way. We now know first hand that as dissimilar as our values, educations, cultures, material trappings, religion and behaviors may be, we are much more alike than we are different.

When we go home, we're not the same persons we were when we started out. We won't stay home for long.

The End

Appendix

TRAVELER RESOURCES

C: COMPANION

▶ **Travel Companion Exchange, Inc (TCE)**
PO Box 833
Amityville NY 11701
Phone: 631-454-0880
Fax: 631-454-0170
www.whytravelalone.com
E-mail:TCE@whytravelalone.com

TCE is the foremost source for finding compatible travel companions. A reputable, respected company for 18 years. Membership includes an informative newsletter. Call, fax, write, or visit their website for information

C: CUSTOMS

▶ **U.S. Customs Service**
1300 Pennsylvania Ave NW
Washington, DC 20229
www.customs.gov
The Customs Service is improving its customer service to international travelers at major U.S. travel hubs by having passenger service reps available to travelers at more than 20 international airports and some seaports where cruise ships dock. Their major purpose is to help travelers clear customs.

The second new service is automated booths or kiosks. All the traveler has to do is type in their country of destination on the self-service computer with a touch screen display and the computer will print the information for you. The screen displays a phone number to call for more information

Customs kiosks are located in the outbound passenger lounges at the following international airports: Atlanta, Boston, Charlotte in NC, Chicago, Dallas/Ft. Worth, Detroit, Houston, JFK in New York, Los Angeles, Miami, Newark in NJ, Philadelphia, San Francisco, San Juan, and Washington/Dulles. More are planned.

D: DISCOUNT TRAVEL SUPPLIERS

▸ **Air Brokers International**
150 Post Street, Ste. 620
San Francisco, CA 94108
800-883-3273
www.airbrokers.com
Request a newsletter, then call and talk to an agent

▸ **Global Adventure Travel**
1849 Willow Pass Road, Ste. 301
Concord, CA 94520
800-888-0686
www.globaladv.com

▸ **High Adventure Travel**
www.airtreks.com
800-350-0612
Obtain ideas and plan an around-the-world trip at this web site and you will be given an estimated cost. Then call an agent to book and/or confirm pricing. More than 40,000 actual or hypothetical itineraries are on this site for examination.

E: EQUIPMENT AND CLOTHES FOR TRAVELERS

▸ **WPC Brands**
1 Rapel Road
Jackson WI 53037
800-558-6614
www.wpcbrands.com
Diabetic supplies for travelers including cold packs. First aid kits for all types of travel and camping meal kits.

▸ **Magellan's**
110 W. Sola Street
Santa Barbara, CA 93101-3007
800-962-4943
Fax: 800-962-4940
www.magellans.com
Call for catalog. Sells a large selection of travel equipment, luggage, travel books, safety items and other accessories.

- **TravelSmith**
  60 Leveroni Court
  Novato CA 94949
  800-950-1600 (Catalog and orders)
  www.travelsmith.com
  A large assortment of easy-care travel clothes and luggage

- **Damart**
  3 Front Street
  Rollinsford NH 03805
  800-258-7300 ·
  Fax: 1-603-742-2050
  www.damart.com
  Call or check website to order free catalog of warm, lightweight garments.

- **Tilley Endurables**
  300 Langner Road
  West Seneca, NY 14244
  800-363- 8737
  www.tilley.com
  Travel/adventure clothing. Free catalog

H: HEALTH INFORMATION
- **IAMAT**
  The International Association for Medical Assistance to Travelers
  417 Center Street, Lewiston NY 14092
  Call: 716-754-4883
  Website: www.sentex.net//~iamat
  E-mail:iamat@sentex.net
  This is a wonderful service for travelers. There is no charge to join but they do ask for a donation to support the organization's work. When you join, they send you a membership card entitling you to a world directory of English-speaking physicians in 550 countries and territories. All doctors have been screened and were educated in English-speaking countries. IAMAT doctors have agreed to a specific fee for office or hotel visits.
  With membership, you also receive a passport sized record for

131

your medical history, a world immunization chart, information about malaria, and other printed material including the sanitary conditions of milk, food and water in many countries.

▸ **Medic-Alert**
2323 Colorado Avenue
Turlock, CA 95382
800-432-5378
www.medicalert.org
Bracelets and necklaces that alert others to your severe allergies, diabetes, or any other medical problem. The bracelets and necklaces have an engraved panel with your information plus a 24-hour hotline that doctors or hospitals can call for more details about your medical condition. The first year cost is $35. Each subsequent year their will be a $15 annual membership fee to keep your medical information updated.

▸ **Medication Tips for Travelers and
The Tenderfeet Traveler**
Order from Newjoy Press. See order form on last page of this book.
Booklets with detailed tips for traveling with medication and travelers' foot care.

▸ **WPC Brands**
1 Rapel Road
Jackson WI 53037
800-558-6614
www.wpcbrands.com
Diabetic supplies for travelers (including cold packs), First aid kits for all types of travel, and camping meal kits.

H: HOSTELLING
▸ **Elderhostel**
PO Box 1959
Wakefield, MA 01180
Toll-free Phone: 877-426-8056
www.elderhostel.org
Educational travel for mature travelers.

- **Hostelling International**
  Forsyth Travel Library, Inc.
  9154 West 57th Street
  Shawnee Mission, KS 66201
  Call 800-367-7984.
  Inexpensive travel for all ages.
  www.iyhf.org/iyhf/ehome.html

H: HOUSE SWAPPING

- **Homelink**
  Call 800-638-3841 or
  www.swapnow.com
  Call or check website for membership costs and information. Five directories, 50 countries

- **Intervac Home Exchange**
  PO Box 590504
  San Francisco, CA 94159
  Call: 800-756-HOME (Leave your name and address to receive an information package.)
  www.intervac.com

- **International Home Exchange Network**
  Exclusively on the Internet. Updated daily. www.ihen.com

I: INSURANCE

- **TripAssist, c/o Access America**
  PO Box 90315
  800-284-8300
  www.accessamerica.com
  Available at AAA offices

- **Medex Insurance Services**
  Trav Med
  9515 Deereco Rd., 4th fl.
  Timonium MD 21093
  Call: 800-732-5309 between 8 a.m. and 4:30 p.m EST
  www.medexassist.com

- **Wallach & Company**
  107 W. Federal Street
  Middleburg, VA 20117
  800-237-6615
  www.wallach.com
  Health and evacuation insurance

- **International SOS Assistance**
  PO Box 11568
  Philadelphia PA 19116
  800-523-8662
  www.internationalsos.com

E: INTERACTIVE TRAVEL OPPORTUNITIES

- **Peace Corps**
  111 20th Street NW
  Washington DC 20526
  800-424-8580
  www.peacecorps.gov./home.html
  Use your life skills to improve the life of disadvantaged peoples.

S: SERVAS

- **U.S. Servas**
  11 John Street
  Suite 407
  New York, NY 10038-4009.
  Website: http://servas.org
  E-mail: servas@servas.org .

  This organization enables hosts willing to invite foreigners into their homes to connect with travelers looking for more contact with local people. Travelers pay a fee to Servas and receive two free nights lodging with each host they visit. Meals may or may not be offered. The organization does not welcome members whose primary motivation for joining is to obtain free rooms. You must be interviewed to join and be sincerely interested in meeting, getting to know, and learning about the culture of citizens in the countries you're visiting..

  George and I recently joined Servas as both hosts and travelers. We are enthusiastic about this organization as a way to

134

promote world understanding. Our travel in Japan and Australia was made infinitely richer by our contact with Servas hosts. As hosts ourselves, we have had four visits with European guests in our New Mexico home.

S: SINGLE TRAVEL
▶ **Connecting Solo Travel**
1996 W. Broadway
Vancouver, B.C. V6J 5C2, Canada
800-557-1757
www. cstn.org
Sample newsletter for $5.

T: TRAIN TRAVEL
▶ **Rail Europe Group (includes BritRail)**
Westchester One
44 South Broadway, 11th floor
White Plains NY 10601
1-800-4-EURAIL
www. raileurope.com

U: U.S. GOVERNMENT RESOURCES
▶ **Center for Disease Control**
800-311-3435
www.cdc.gov
Information about immunizations needed for world travel, health conditions in the world, health warnings and much more. See their web site.

▶ **Consular Information Sheets, Travel Warnings and Public Announcements** may be heard anytime by dialing 202-647-5225 from a touch tone phone or by visiting their website: http://travel.state.gov/travel_warnings.html

▶ **U.S. State Department, Consular Affairs Publications**
Available for sale from the Superintendent of Documents
U.S. Government Printing Office
Washington DC 20402

Phone 202-512-1800 for prices and availability.

A Safe Trip Abroad contains helpful precautions one can take to minimize the chance of becoming a victim of terrorism or crime.

Travel Tips for Older Americans contains special health, safety and travel information for older Americans.

Your Trip Abroad offers tips on obtaining a passport, consider ations in preparing for your trip, and other sources of information.

► **Backgound Notes** are brief, factual pamphlets describing the countries of the world. They contain current information on each country's people, culture, geography, history, government, economy, and political conditions. Single copies may be ordered from the U.S. Government Printing Office, Washington DC 20402. You can also order *Background Notes* from the internet site at: http://www.state.gov/www/background_notes/index.html

NOTE: Other publications are available from the GPO. See www.travel.state.gov

THE U.S.GOVERNMENT AND DISASTER ABROAD

Most persons travel safely and have wonderful experiences. Individuals can usually handle minor crises with foresight and common sense. However, it always pays to be informed and prepared so that if you are caught up in one of the rare instances when a disaster occurs, you will know what to do. Assess your situation and surroundings wherever you are. Try to maintain a healthy balance in the zone between complacency and paranoia.

The U.S. State Department recommends that you inform the U.S. embassy or consulate when you arrive in a foreign country. It is important to know the address and phone number of the embassy and what they do for U.S. citizens abroad.

Note: Detailed information about the State Department's services are on the Internet at http://travel.state.gov. You can print information, warnings, booklets, and access other government agencies such as the Center for Disease Control.

The following table gives an overview of the state department's set up for services to citizens overseas.

United States Department of State

⇓

Bureau of Consular Affairs

⇓

Overseas Citizen Services

⇓ ⇓ ⇓

American Citizens Services and Crises Mgmt	Office of Children's Services	Office of Policy Review & Interagency Liaison

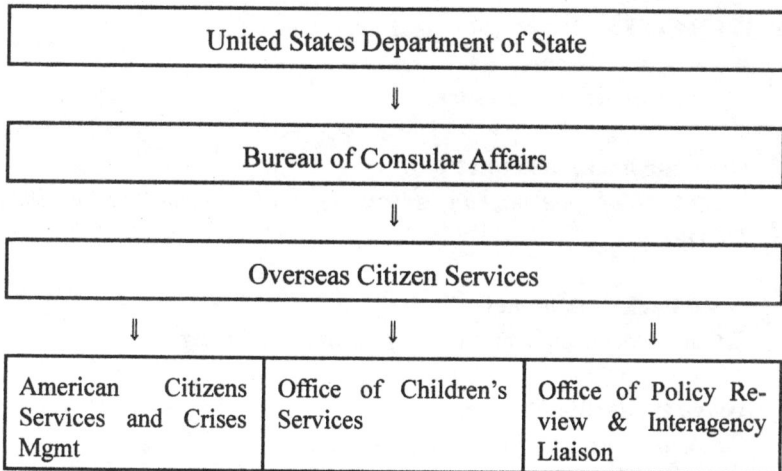

Overseas Citizens Services in the State Department's Bureau of Consular Affairs is responsible for the welfare and whereabouts of U.S. citizens traveling and residing abroad. It has three offices:

1. **American Citizens Services and Crisis Management** assists in all matters involving protective services for Americans abroad, including arrests, death cases, financial or medical emergencies, and welfare and whereabouts inquiries. The office also issues Travel Warnings and Consular Information Sheets and provides guidance in many other areas.

Note: Travel warnings are issued when the State Department advises citizens to defer travel to a country because of dangerous conditions or because the U.S. has no diplomatic relations with the country.

Consular Information Sheets contain information on entry requirements, crime and security conditions, areas of instability and other details about travel in a particular country.

2. **The Office of Children's Issues** formulates, develops and coordinates policies and programs on international parental child abduction and international adoptions.
3. **The Office of Policy Review and Interagency Liaison** provides guidance on laws, documentation of Americans living abroad. It offers advice about treaties and agreements and legislative matters.

137

W: WEB SITES

▶ **www.trailwalk.com**
Online magazine for trekkers

▶ **www.the backpacker.net**
Directory of backpacking resources and information on the internet

▶ **www.backpacking.net**
Site with lots of information on packing and hiking.

▶ **www. thebackpacker.com**
Site with tools and tips for backpackers

BOOK LIST

Berman, Eleanor. *Traveling Solo: Advice and Ideas for More than 250 Great Vacations.*Globe Pequot Press, 1997.

*Lynn, Cynthia. *No More Hotels in Paris: How to Find Alternative Accommodations.* Ventura, CA: Newjoy Press, 1999. Updated 5/2000

*Lynn, Cynthia. *No More Hotels in Rome: How to Find Alternative Accommodations.* Ventura, CA: Newjoy Press, 2000.

McMillon, Bill. *Volunteer Vacations: Short Term Adventures That Will Benefit You and Others.* Chicago. Chicago Review Press, 1997.

*Nyquist, Joy. *Travel Light: How to Go Anywhere in the World With Only One Suitcase.* Ventura, CA: Newjoy Press, 2000.

*Shearer, Clive. *Create Your Own European Adventure: Leave the Guidebooks at Home.* Ventura, CA: Newjoy Press,1999.

Schroeder, Dirk G. *Staying Healthy in Asia, Africa, and Latin America.* Moon Publications, 2000. $10.75.
Order from Amazon.com

Wingler, Sharon. *Travel Alone and Love It: A Flight Attendant's Guide to Solo Travel.* Chicago. Chicago Spectrum Press, 1997.

Order the following guidebooks from amazon.com or look for them at your local bookstores.

Lonely Planet Guides
Moon Handbooks
Insight Compact Guides
Rough Guides
Berkeley Guides

*Convenient ordering from Newjoy Press. See page 147.

INDEX

143

ORDER FORM

Please send me the following books:

#	BOOK TITLE	Price	Total
	The Tenderfeet Traveler (booklet)	$3.00	
	Medication Tips for Travelers (booklet)	$3.00	
	NEWJOY PRESS CATALOG	**FREE**	
	Postage & Handling Each book $1.80 Each additional book add 35 cents Orders of 10 or more books invoiced separately. Priority , UPS, Express mail - extra fee	Subtotal	
		*Tax	
		P&H	
		TOTAL	

California residents pay 7.25% sales tax

√ **Mail this form with check or credit card number**
√ **Call: 800-876-1373**
√ **Fax: 805-9840503**

Card No._____ ___ ___ ___ ___ ___ ___ ___ ___ ___ ___ ___ ___ ___ ___

Signature_____Exp. Date_____
    □ Visa   □ MasterCard   □ American Express   □ Check

Please print clearly

Name: _____

Address _____

City, State, Zip _____

Phone (   )_____

Newjoy Press, PO Box 3437, Ventura CA 93006

Thank you for your order

Guarantee
If, for any reason, you are not satisfied with your purchase,
simply return it in resaleable condition
and your money will be refunded.